I Can't Believe You Went Through My Stuff!

HOW TO GIVE YOUR TEENS THE PRIVACY THEY CRAVE AND THE GUIDANCE THEY NEED

PETER L. SHERAS, PH.D.,
WITH ANDREA THOMPSON

A SKYLIGHT PRESS BOOK
A FIRESIDE BOOK
PUBLISHED BY SIMON & SCHUSTER
New York   London   Toronto   Sydney

FIRESIDE
Rockefeller Center
1230 Avenue of the Americas
New York, NY 10020

FIRESIDE and colophon are registered trademarks
of Simon & Schuster, Inc.

"A Skylight Press book."

For information regarding special discounts for bulk purchases,
please contact Simon & Schuster Special Sales at 1-800-456-6798
or business@simonandschuster.com

Designed by Jan Pisciotta

Manufactured in the United States of America

10   9   8   7   6   5   4   3   2   1

Library of Congress Cataloging-in-Publication Data
Sheras, Peter L.
  I can't believe you went through my stuff! : how to give your teens the privacy
    they crave and the guidance they need/Peter L. Sheras with Andrea Thompson.
      p. cm.
    "A Skylight Press book."
    "A Fireside book."
    Includes index.
1.Parent and teenager. 2. Parenting. 3. Adolescent psychology. 4. Secrecy.
I. Thompson, Andrea (Andrea B.) II. Title.
HQ799.15.S56   2004
649'.125—dc22   2004045409

ISBN 0-7432-5215-2

ACKNOWLEDGMENTS

This book is a labor of love for me. I acknowledge the contributions of all those teenagers and families that have trusted me with their lives and experiences over the years. I have learned from them beyond measure. I especially thank my own children, Dan and Sarah, who have been my greatest teachers and inspiration. Finally, to my wife, colleague, and co-parent, Phyllis, I extend my gratitude for her tireless support, great insight, and loving partnership.

CONTENTS

Preface

In my writing and lecturing, I approach the teaching tasks with the attitude of a scientist telling good stories: Here's what happened, and here, according to our current understanding, is why it happened. This book includes many stories of adolescents and their parents. In each case, for the sake of privacy, names and other specific details do not correspond to those of real individuals I have counseled. Their stories, however, are grounded in my clinical experience and research. Over my three decades of working with children and families, the common themes that make adolescence a trying time for parent and child alike have emerged. Those themes determined the shape of this book.

Psychologists often don't want to state an interpretation of behavior or a recommendation for action until we're absolutely sure we have the thing right. The truth is, we know enough to be helpful. My job is to translate what we think we know about children into information that's genuinely useful to a parent, and that's what I hope you will find in *I Can't Believe You Went Through My Stuff!*

CHAPTER 1

Secrets and Privacy

How Your Teenager Starts Answering the Question "Who Am I?"

When your child was little, he probably loved it when you sat on his bed and read him a story or just talked. Now, he's eleven or twelve or fifteen, and you're hearing some version of, "Please get out of my room. Why do you always come in here?" When you asked your young child what she and her friend watched on TV that afternoon, she told you. Now you hear some version of, "That's private. Why do you want to know, anyway?" And you're caught up short: *What? My sweet child has undergone this metamorphosis from nice to nasty, from good to not so good, from known to unknown, and I'm just doing what I've always done.*

Here's something I've noticed in my thirty years as a clinical psychologist working with adolescents, and as a father myself: Parents are not aware they can't just keep using the same approaches and skills they employed when their children were younger. Once a parent, always a parent is true enough—but when your child enters the preteen and teen years, what you did by instinct in years past doesn't necessarily work or go over very well. In some situations, it's the exact opposite of what in the long run is most helpful for your child.

I call this rude awakening the beginning, ideally, of your shift into Stage 2 parenting. Your child is changing in new ways; you need to change right along with him. And secrets—his craving for privacy, his ferocious insistence on running his own life—is probably the biggest aspect of that shift in orientation.

There's good news and bad news—actually, it's all good news, for reasons I'll explain and as I hope this book will make clear.

The good news: Keeping secrets from you is a normal—more than normal, *necessary*—aspect of your teenager's development. It's a healthy part of the construction of his identity, or how he figures out who he is. You should relish that drive and nurture it.

The bad news: Keeping some secrets from you contributes to a parent/child relationship that without question adds to your load of worry and aggravation. The Stage 2 mind-set isn't always effortlessly maintained. But with some smart, workable strategies under your belt—the strategies I describe here—you will feel empowered to be the kind of parent your child needs you to be during these transition years.

When I say parenting changes, I'm not talking about a 180-degree about-face in the way you interact with your son or daughter. You are still the parent; he or she is still the child. You have both powers and responsibilities that he or she does not have. As you'll see in the following chapters, shifting into Stage 2 means:

- You'll listen to your child a little more, and maybe talk a little less yourself.

- You'll recognize the questions you ask that suddenly sound to your child like obnoxious prying into his private life, and you'll refrain from asking them (some of them, anyway).

- You'll stay informed about what your child is up to, without embarrassing or infuriating her and driving her farther underground.

- You'll allow your child the freedom to take the risks she needs to take in order to grow, and you'll see how to step in when the risks are getting *too* risky.

- You'll be able to convey your opinions, beliefs, and knowledge of the world, in a way that doesn't cause him to feel you're telling him what to think and how to live.

Adolescence is stressful—sometimes overwhelming—for both teen and parent, but it's also a rich, rewarding, fascinating time. When you think about it objectively, if you can manage to, what could be more interesting than being on the scene as your boy or girl takes some giant strides toward adulthood?

Building an identity is the main challenge of your adolescent's life. It's a challenge that helps shed light on the "Get out of my room!" syndrome.

Who Am I?: Your Teen's Quest for Identity

This is the question your child is trying to answer. "Who am I?" first shows up at the beginning of adolescence. Before then, children are self-referential but not very self-conscious; they play but they don't *watch* themselves playing. Starting around age eleven or twelve, however, they begin to reflect on themselves in earnest and become acutely aware of how they look, feel, think, act, walk, sit, smell, and sound. They're also suddenly interested in how others are taking them in, sort of like seeing with a third eye—*I'm observing myself and observing the way others observe me.* (This is when Sally calls the cute boy to talk about Emily, while Emily is in Sally's house listening in on the extension. These plots are hatched expressly to meet the child's need to find out how others perceive her.)

"Who am I?" (or "How, exactly, am I unique or special and not like everyone else?") is the umbrella question that encompasses many others, and the questions become deeper or harder or more sophisticated as a child moves along from preteen to full-blown adolescent.

- What are my opinions about religion and politics, about what's right and what's wrong, about food, fashion, and music, about animal rights and the salaries these pro athletes get?

- What sort of people do I want to spend time with, and why?

- What kind of work should I do someday, what would I be good at?

- What kind of sexual being am I?

- What do I want out of life?

Undeniably, such questions reflect a child's struggle to be an individual, a person in his own right, to actually experience a sense of his existence. Your child is likely to come up with answers (always subject to adjustment the next day, week, or month) in various ways: by experimenting with different behaviors, by trying on alternate responses to all the day-to-day situations he encounters; by asking friends for information and looking to friends as models, by seeking external validation from the world of peers. (I remember myself in middle school one day, happening to be walking down the hall with a bunch of the cool kids, and thinking, *Here I am, walking down the hall with cool kids. I must be a cool kid.*)

He also spends time thinking and brooding, constructing a sort of separate place where he can go, to be himself in his own head.

The resource he's *not* so likely to look to for answers is his parents.

For your child, the "Who am I?" years of course include many "firsts": first kiss, first boyfriend/girlfriend, first sampling of an alcoholic beverage, perhaps first brush with a law enforcement official. You may remember with fondness the original firsts in your child's life: first step, first words, first day at kindergarten, first time he tied his shoelaces by himself. While the latest markers on his road to maturity are just as significant, this time around you probably won't hear much about them at all. He doesn't want you to.

To your adolescent's way of thinking, there are legitimate reasons to keep Mom and Dad in the dark.

Why Your Child Has a Secret Life

If your teen could (and felt inclined to) offer some explanations for "Get out of my room!" here's what she might come up with:

I don't want to tell my parents what I'm doing and thinking because . . .

. . . they'll try to stop me and or totally freak out and/or want to know everything about my life.

Your thirteen-year-old wants to meet her boyfriend at the mall, but she believes that if she mentions the plan at home, first, you'll react with dismay and horror that she has a boyfriend at all, and second, you'll come up with five reasons why the mall meeting is not going to happen. So she tells you she's getting together with her two girlfriends, which is partly true because her friends might also show up at the mall. This makes sense to her. It also doesn't seem terribly dishonest. One of the subjects I get to later in this book is the adolescent lie and the fact that teens usually lie or keep some bit of business a secret from their parents simply because they don't want to be stopped from doing something they have in mind.

But as adolescents are developing this sense of privacy, many typically come to feel they can't communicate with their parents about *anything*. The notion is, *If I tell you about my school grades, then the next thing is you're going to want to know who I'm friends with or what's in my desk drawer. And that's intolerable. So I'm not going to tell you anything.*

In this atmosphere, an innocent-sounding (to your ears) observation or question often feels to your child as if you're determined to superimpose your values on her. She wants to come up with her own values (which may turn out to be the same as yours, but you didn't lay them on her). She might also be quick to decide you're speaking out of both sides of your mouth, and she wants to squelch the conversation entirely—or at least, she's not about to believe everything you say. You mention, "Polly, how did you do on the math test? I bet you did great, because I know how important it is to you to be a good student, and I'm only asking because I have your best interests in mind." Polly thinks, *Oh, yeah? Don't be such a hypocrite, Mom. You mean it reflects well on you with all your little friends when I get good grades, and that's what you're really thinking about.*

. . . they don't understand, they don't really know me.

One part of "You don't really know me" is "I am not like you."

If you tell your nine-year-old he's a chip off the old block, he beams with pride. Tell that to your thirteen-year-old, and he's insulted. He's insulted not because he hates how you are; he just thinks it's presumptuous and wrong of you to think you know all about him (which is true—you don't). And he senses, *If I'm an open book to my parents, if they know all about me, I'm not really myself, not an independent being with my own identity.* In adolescence, as hormones are raging and cognitive processes become more sophisticated, children perceive themselves as greatly more complex beings than they were just a little while ago. And they are, in fact, more complex. So many of the interactions in which teens push parents away arise from that notion, "You don't understand." Of course, the subtext is, "I don't understand myself. But don't tell me *you* know what's going on with me."

In fact, the quickest, easiest answer to "Who am I?" is, "I am not my parents. I will be or do the opposite of what they are or do." The adolescent can't be like Mom or Dad, because then she's not differentiating or distinguishing herself. Your child says, "You're a Republican, Dad? Okay, I'm a Democrat." "You eat meat, Mother. That's disgusting, I'm a vegetarian." (Brief bouts with vegetarianism, by the way, which start off by wanting to be different from parents and also thinking of all the baby lambs, are extremely common among adolescents. Often, the bout is over when the child considers the vegan distinction: "You mean I can't have an egg? Well, I didn't really want to go *that* far.")

The thing is, being or doing the opposite of Mom or Dad confers instant identity. Easy as pie.

I don't want to ask my parents about some stuff that's happening because . . .

. . . it would be too hideously, totally embarrassing . . .

Physiological developments over these years are traumatic. Sprouting body hair, growing breast buds, the beginning of menstruation, undescended testicles, overall changes in physique—suddenly preteens or teens are terribly confused about their bodies. Usually, they're not quite sure what's going on, or what to look for or expect. Many questions arise, and they're profoundly embarrassing ones to ask any adult. Trips to the pediatrician become highly stressful and mortifying.

Sexual feelings fall in the same category. Experiencing sexual arousal, *worrying* about sexual arousal, early physical contacts with a first boyfriend or girlfriend—all these generally are matters a young teen is loathe to talk about with Mom or Dad. A scene in Phillip Roth's novel *Portnoy's Complaint* put a funny spin on a boy's obsessive concern with masturbating and fears that his penis will fall off. Young Portnoy fantasizes while standing in the kitchen that his penis drops down his pants leg to the floor due to excessive masturbation. His mother is saying, "What's that?" as he attempts to kick the offending organ behind the refrigerator and out of sight. It's part of an adolescent's worry: I have no idea what's happening, but whatever it is, *my mother must not know about it.*

Then, too, this is the age when your child is trying so hard to demonstrate that she doesn't need you. Telling you difficult stuff, even if she's desperate for information or reassurance, would imply that she really does need you after all.

... my friends know what's what, my parents don't.

About bodily changes, new sexual feelings, and much else she wants to know, where does a child go for information? Usually to her friends.

Starting around age eleven or twelve for boys, a little earlier for girls, children turn away from parents (not entirely, of course) and grow toward their peers. Close friendships—Harry Stack Sullivan, a father of American psychiatry, called them "chumships"—are often part of the picture at these ages. This enhanced importance of social relationships hinges on the development of empathy; just as children gain higher levels of moral reasoning and intellectual abilities, they also progress emotionally. Suddenly, the child develops the interest and ability to imagine what someone else is feeling. It enables her to find people who feel the same way she does, which strikes a blow against the increasing sense of isolation young teens experience as they push off from Mom and Dad. Girls tend to be more intellectual and verbal, boys more physical. For both, chumships are powerful connections, with feelings of closeness and camaraderie that weren't there before.

I remember a day when my daughter was about twelve and had a friend sleep over. The following morning, after her friend left, my daughter sat there, wide-eyed and thoughtful. She said, "I never had an experience like that before. Everything I said had happened to her or she was thinking about it too. I felt like she's the first person who really understands me."

But in addition to feeling liked, understood, and accepted (an important stage in the development of identity, other people seeing that you exist), adolescents look to their peers to learn what the correct thing is.

Your child wants to do the correct thing, and she's pretty sure you can't tell her what that would be. Social psychologists talk about this as the creation of social reality: When matters begin to become physically (and in other ways) confusing, when the facts are not clear, we look for consensus to help us decide what to do. For your young teen, an innocuous example might be, "What's a cool thing to wear?" Her friends will give her an answer, one that has nothing to do with any fact. As a parent, you might say, "Well, a cool thing to wear is what we can afford to buy for you." That's a fact, but it's not a helpful fact to your child.

I want to hang out in my own room and not be around my parents so much because . . .

. . . my parents kind of gross me out.

Adolescents don't want to be dependent on their parents. Since they are, as they realize ruefully, bound to rely on Mom and Dad for big things like a roof over their head, money, food, clothes, and the family car, they seize on the small ways by which they can physically detach—don't want to go on vacation together, don't want to go out to dinner together. They really wish to be away from those two individuals.

At the same time, teens may begin to observe aspects of Mom and Dad that they find annoying, maybe slightly repugnant.

During these years, your child experiences a heightened sensitivity to everyone and everything. As she's becoming more self-conscious about her own mannerisms, she's also more aware of everybody else's, including the habits of her friends and of her parents. Characteristics she barely perceived before she now has intense feelings about—this or that is *totally* gross! (Just plain "gross" isn't sufficient to describe the level of disgust.)

When a teen begins to notice these aspects of her parents, she compares them to an ideal image, and Mom and Dad fall far short of the ideal. In their classic study *Being Adolescent*, researchers Mihaly Csikszentmihalyi and Reed Larson observed, "Much tension in the family results from the way parents eat, dress, talk or blow their noses. Teenagers feel they are stuck with having to pay attention to irritating mannerisms over which they have no control." They add, "Becoming independent means having a choice over what one pays attention to."

So parents come off the pedestal a little: "You were supposed to be perfect, Mom, but guess what? You're not! Now I see that you slurp your soup, and it makes me want to puke, and I would never eat like that."

It bolsters her argument that she is and should be different from her parents. It contributes to "Get out of my room!"

. . . I need to explore and think.

The bedroom is the sanctuary, a safe haven, a retreat from the stresses of the day, a place to be removed from the folks for a while.

Images in the pop culture, on TV, and in the movies often depict teenagers in their room "multitasking": simultaneously on the computer, blasting music, and talking on the phone. Sometimes your child might fit in that picture. Sometimes he might be in his room not doing much of anything at all, which typically gives a parent fits. A boy in one of my groups said he likes to lie on his bed playing with his old Slinky, just rolling it back and forth from one hand to the other: "For some reason, this makes my mom nervous. She thinks there's something wrong with me. I'd close the door, but we have this open-door policy in my house, so I can't do that. But there's nothing really wrong. The Slinky just helps me to think."

Adolescents are kind of blossoming into this notion of being independent beings; they're capable of abstract thinking and believe they're capable of their own ideas and opinions. There's a lot of soul-searching going on. Sometimes your child just wants to be left alone to do that.

The Challenge of Stage 2 Parenting

The strategies I talk about in the following chapters touch on all these ways adolescents play out their need to have secrets, and on the appropriate responses you should make. Generally speaking, they revolve around the two essential and somewhat contrasting ingredients in Stage 2 parenting.

Know when to step back.

Nurture your child's quest for identity.

The theorist Erik Erikson wrote persuasively about identity formation as the main task of the adolescent years. John Marcia and other researchers further developed the theme and described possible outcomes when an individual fails at or inadequately embraces the struggle. He or she may fall into an identity status called "foreclosure": The teen seems to have come up with answers to "Who am I?" but in fact hasn't thought things through, tried out various personae, or grappled with different ways of being. He picks a path or an idea for the sake of achieving a recognizable identity, or maybe for the sake of getting Mom and Dad off his back ("I'll be a doctor because my mother is a doctor" or "I grew up Greek Orthodox and my parents are Greek Orthodox, so that's just what I am"). It's going through the motions, and it's an identity that won't necessarily cause him to feel happy. Later on, as an adult, that can make life difficult.

Conversely, the parent who says, "This is how it's going to be around here, like it or lump it," can paint an adolescent into a corner, perhaps forcing him to be indirect or devious. He might then take extreme measures to construct identities that are either dangerous or completely unacceptable in some way.

It's so important to nurture your child's quest for identity, which means, in part, allowing him privacy and the safe and sacred and secret places in which he can grow.

Know when to step in.

Think on your feet and think ahead.

Adolescence may be the first time a child has the autonomy to do dangerous things. A teen's ability to perform outstrips her ability to understand, which can create the illusion in her own mind of being more adult than she is. It's often easy for her to maintain that illusion: Your thirteen-year-old daughter can buy clothes and cosmetics that make her look like a nineteen-year-old. And the world, in some ways, treats her as a nineteen-year-old, although developmentally she's not equipped to deal with that response.

Our culture also expects teenagers to be more advanced than they are, to act like adults without really teaching them to be adults. It's convenient, in a sense, to declare certain turning points: You're sixteen, you can drive; eighteen, you can buy cigarettes; twenty-one, okay, now you can drink. But there's little notion of running up to those markers and seeing if an adolescent is really ready—if he knows what he needs to know to move on to maturity.

So far, I've been emphasizing what's different about Stage 2 parenting, but some aspects remain the same, including your need and responsibility to keep your child safe and to teach him what he needs to know, just as you always have. Which means checking in, keeping the dialogue going, offering suggestions. The difference now is, he doesn't want you to. My dog once had an ear infection. Every time I went to put drops in his ears, he tried to bite me. And I didn't blame him. But I put in the drops anyway. You will do the equivalent with your son or daughter, without being deterred or upset by his or her wish sometimes to bite.

As you keep checking in in the ways I describe throughout this book, often over your adolescent's objections, it's necessary to think on your feet and think ahead—in order to figure out which dangerous behaviors are a passing phase and which look as if they might be sticking. Many parents as a matter of course sort of deal with whatever comes up, when it comes up; taking a more proactive stance is better for your child, including making some of the thinking-ahead strategies I describe part of your parent/child relationship.

In short, you will, I hope, pick up in these pages some good ideas on how to treat your adolescent as the grown-up he wants to be, while protecting and guiding him as the growing child you know he, in many ways, still is.

Your Unique Child

I have been talking about "your child" as if one prototypical adolescent exists: one size fits all. Of course, this isn't the case. Your child is not necessarily like other children. Your son probably isn't like his brother or his sister. How your teen navigates the quest for identity and carries on his secret life is influenced by a number of factors, including the kind of parenting he receives, his peers, his neighborhood or culture, and, significantly, his personality or characteristics of temperament.

Some children are sort of inward or introverted. Others are more active or extroverted. Some are quiet and thoughtful, some reactive, some impulsive. Your teen probably falls into one or another broad category, and you surely have a notion of what that is after living with her for the last twelve, thirteen, or fourteen years. The onset of adolescence doesn't mean your son or daughter abruptly sheds all resemblance to the little kid he or she once was.

However, I urge you to resist too much "typing"—or labeling or diagnosing—of your child. Labeling can interfere with what's needed during Stage 2 parenting, because the minute you type your child, you stop listening and observing; you view the evidence differently (*Aha! He's always been an introvert, so that's why he doesn't want to leave his room* or *Aha! He's always been a rebellious type, so that's why he didn't come home last night*).

Children differ from one another. It's also true, however, that adolescents are moving targets. Developmentally, healthy teens are so actively in transition that they're constantly trying on (or overcome by) a variety of moods and attitudes, postures and behaviors. Your child might want to stick right next to you for twenty minutes and have you tickle her neck. Then maybe she's aloof and seemingly depressed for the next hour and a half, then bouncing off the walls for the next week.

It's also the case, as recent research is demonstrating, that a child's brain is changing during adolescence, with a dramatic increase in the number of synapses and an explosion of neural activity that means he's making new connections on a nanosecond-to-nanosecond basis. So we now believe there is some biological underpinning for a teen's emotional lability;

he might look confused or spacey sometimes, or show bad judgment, and it's at least partly a result of the brain firing as a function of its normal development.

The message for any parent: Keep listening, keep responding, and keep letting your teen know that you're in his corner.

When I work with a family, I usually meet first with the parent or parents and the child together, then with the parents alone, finally with the child alone. I have a guiding rule, which I explain at the outset to all involved: "Mom and Dad, everything your child tells me I will not reveal to you, except if it's legally binding on me to do so. Everything you tell me about your child, I will reveal to your child." My aim is to ensure that the child, my client, is not suspicious about the process we're embarking on and knows I'm not going to spill the beans to her mother behind her back. My guiding rule facilitates the notion that I'm on her side. In a sense, I try to abandon an adult posture and to convey the idea that I'm not here to reprimand, but to ask "What's happening?" and "Can I help?"

And in a sense, that's one of your challenges in Stage 2 parenting. You need to abandon your I-am-the-adult, you-are-the-child mind-set. You are there not to pry or to judge, but to say, "What's going on with you, my much-loved son/daughter? And remember, I'm on your side." Which does *not* mean that you offer no opinions, set no boundaries, impose no consequences, or take no actions when your child may be flirting with danger.

My aim is not to tell you exactly what to do. Rather, my aim is to outline an overall approach to dealing with your teen's secret life, one that will help you escape the two extremes the Stage 2 parent can so easily fall into: out of frustration, annoyance, and/or worry, either demanding information about everything an adolescent is up to (and upsetting his developmental need for privacy) or, on the other hand, ignoring everything he's up to (and just looking the other way and hoping for the best).

Before we begin, I want to turn myself in a little. I'm not an expert. I do have experience, but the only expert on your child is you. The best I can do is tell you what I have learned from knowing and working with thousands of adolescents over the years and from being a father myself. But you're going to have to make up your mind about many issues as they come along. And you know what? You will fail sometimes; you'll say the wrong thing or take the wrong tack. Some of the failures will be hilarious; some will be frightening. Not entering the fray, however, is the biggest failure. So let's get in there.

The Shift to Stage 2 Parenting

Knowing Yourself and the Limits of Your Power

Knowing your limits—that is, what you reasonably can and cannot expect to learn and control about your child's life—begins with this understanding: During the transition age, your child no longer perceives you as a benign authority figure but as a wielder of power.

Younger children give their parents a great deal of authority—to feed them, take care of them, plan their days—without consciously thinking about it all. The contract from young child to parent is, essentially: *I'll let you take over and in return I'll get a lot back.* In the preteen and teen years, your child starts viewing your contributions to her life not as a sign of appropriate and welcome authority but as a display of raw power. Here's what's going on in her mind: *Mother, I never told you to put my underwear in the drawer, straighten up my room, make meat loaf for dinner, say hello to my friends. Who said you could do that? You're just doing it because you can, because you want to make my life miserable, and you don't want me to do what I want to do.*

There *you* are, going along as always, straightening up her room and making meat loaf. Once you were appreciated; now you're accused of being a tyrant.

The transition starts around age eleven or twelve, as your

child's mind changes. Last week everything was okay; today everything's wrong. One day he says, "Thanks for making my lunch, Mom." The next day: "Oh, God, I don't want this disgusting stuff again."

There's an old joke that underscores the seeming abruptness of this monumental shift. Jonathan is a healthy boy but he never talks. His parents hire tutors, send him to speech experts, and enroll him in special schools. Still, Jonathan never talks. One morning when he's about thirteen, Jonathan says, "I hate oatmeal." His parents are astonished and aghast. "What?" they say. "You can talk? All these years, all that money we spent on you, and all along you could talk? How come you never said anything?" Jonathan replies, "Well, so far everything's been okay."

Of course, there's no such razor's edge distinction. Children go back and forth for a few years; do the same thing three days in a row and maybe you'll get three completely different reactions to your efforts. And yet parents often describe the "overnight" change in their child. That's how it feels to them.

Along with a general air of disapproval directed at you, your child is suddenly secretive about what's going on with her and often unwilling to let you in on even the most mundane aspects of her days. She also begins insisting on what may sometimes seem to you a ridiculous degree of privacy: Her room, her closet, her desk drawers, her phone conversations with friends are all off-limits. As a parent, you need to adopt a different kind of attitude yourself, one that respects her developmental need to keep some of her life hers. Here, I want to suggest some ways you can, practically speaking, create an overall atmosphere that maintains connectedness and is tolerable to your child.

It includes recognizing uncomfortable feelings you're probably experiencing and learning to manage them.

Be prepared to feel a little sad about your changing lot in your child's life.

This is hard to accept: Many of your adolescent's activities take place outside of your control, even outside of your awareness. Her most profound experiences—social rejection, first sexual encounters, the pressure to take drugs or drink alcohol with friends—will occur when you're not there to protect her, no matter how vigilant you are. She also may be telling you little about them (remember all the things you never told your parents).

That fact creates fear in your mind over your child's health and safety. You're worried that she'll be in danger or that she's not ready or able to make good decisions. And indeed, adolescents are often unprepared for the challenges they are facing. But something else is going on during this transition as well: It's painfully clear that your child is separating from you and the family. She is no longer regularly seeking comfort from you. She no longer wants or needs your input in many ways. In one sense, you're proud of her; in another, you're grieving. She's letting go of you, you're letting go of her, and that's not easy.

Of course, the letting-go process really began years earlier, perhaps when you dropped your three-year-old off for his first day at preschool—and you, not he, broke into tears at the separation. One mother remembered episodes of mini-grieving over the years, starting when her daughter was seven months old. "That's when I stopped breast-feeding," she said, "and I was so sad. It was truly one of those my-baby's-growing-up moments. At age seven months! Then, of course, there turned out to be many, many more moments over the thirteen years since that day."

The process continues in incremental stages. But the first time your daughter goes away with a friend's family for the weekend and doesn't want your help packing her overnight bag or the first time your son announces he won't be home for dinner much this week underscores the reality that your child is moving into a life that isn't going to involve you in the same old ways. Along with the pride and the worries, there's sadness. It's normal. What matters is that you do not allow those feelings to cause you to cling to your child in a manner he's bound to resent, or to react in anger and hurt when she's telling you to please get out of her room now.

You cannot stop your child from growing up.

As dearly as you might wish to keep the days of childlike innocence going a bit longer, your son or daughter is moving on. Everyone will ease into the transition more successfully if you start early to acknowledge the changing scene.

If you're the parent of a ten- or eleven-year-old, that's a great time to indicate that you know, as your child is starting to know, that things are going to be evolving over the coming years. The nature of your communication will change, largely because of that shift in your child's mind that causes him to perceive you as a power-mad manipulator of his life. He's much more likely to question your decisions, much more likely to take your words and actions as an assertion of your control over him and your wish to keep him in check, rather than as the behavior of a benevolent provider. And you'll be entering the often thorny territory of your child driving the car, going to parties in strange homes, and other activities that require negotiations, curfews, consequences, and so on.

It's an excellent idea to say to your preteen, before any major issues are surfacing, something like, "Well, we're approaching a time, kiddo, you and us, when you're going to be a lot more independent. You're going to be away from home more often, more into activities that don't involve us. And we, your parents, are going to have to get used to that. We're going to have to try doing some things a little differently. You and us, we'll figure it out together as we go along."

That's the gist of the message, anyway. I often tell children that their parents are going through changes too, that they're arriving at new understandings and they're doing the best they can in their own way. "Just give them a little time to work it out," I say, "they'll get over it." Everyone needs to be prepared, and as a parent, you can let your child know that you'll be trying to remember he's not entirely your little baby anymore.

That is not to say, of course, that if age ten or eleven has come and gone without you starting a new dialogue, you've lost your one window of opportunity and the case is closed.

You may be behind the times . . . by a week.

Laura, age eleven, adored ballet. She'd taken lessons, loved to attend live performances, and had her favorite superstars in the local dance company. For her twelfth birthday, her parents bought her an exquisite coffee-table book on ballet. Laura seemed less than thrilled and barely gave it a glance. "What's this?" her mother said. "I thought you love ballet." "No, it's kind of stupid," Laura said.

Adam's parents wanted to redo their basement, turning it into a guest room. But fourteen-year-old Adam was seriously into weight lifting and had persuaded his father to set him up with equipment that took over the space. He spent the summer ferociously working out downstairs. One fall day his mother made a passing observation at dinner that maybe when Adam left for college in a few years they'd put his gym equipment in the garage and fix up the basement for guests. "Oh, you can get rid of that stuff now if you want," Adam said. "Have a yard sale."

When this kind of abrupt switch happens, parents typically are startled. You prepare your daughter's favorite blueberry pancakes, and she says, "Pancakes? You know I hate pancakes!" "What do you mean, you've always loved pancakes," you point out. "Oh, please," she says disdainfully, "all those carbohydrates, give me a break!" It can seem as if a child is simply being contrary on purpose. In fact, children's tastes, interests, and opinions do change, sometimes radically, over these years, and parents don't realize that they've sort of stopped tracking them.

Keep yourself up to date about your child. One way of keeping connected to your increasingly mysterious child is to ask yourself, "How well do I know this kid, right now? Do I know his best friend? His favorite sport? His favorite TV show? His favorite teacher? Do I know what things embarrass him? What things make him laugh?"

Parents will say, "Of course I know my own child!" Their children reply, "No way!" It's also true that a teen doesn't *want* his parents to know all this stuff because if they did, it would mean he's very transparent and predictable—basically the same little boy he always was and not his own person. So he keeps it secret. But you can gain such information just by observing and listening and adjusting your perceptions as your child moves along. Allow him to inform you. You might say, "I'd like to make your favorite dinner, and what would that be?"

Keeping up to date makes it more likely that when your child actually needs your advice or suggestions, what you have to say won't be coming from somewhere out in left field.

Sometimes you must share a lot to get a little in return.

There will always be a limit to how much you'll hear from your child about his secret life, especially the negative or worrisome feelings and behaviors. But one way to help him feel more willing and/or comfortable about letting you in on details is to offer your own imperfections for his inspection.

Let your child begin to see you as a separate human being. Talk about yourself, how *your* day went. Maybe share some of your personal horror stories. When your child was younger, you probably elected not to expose yourself in these ways *(I had a terrible day at the office . . . I'm in trouble with one of my clients . . . Looks like we're getting an IRS audit)*. You wanted to appear perfect to your child, and that's fine. When she's a little older, your self-revelations—especially where you're screwing up—are just what's likely to appeal to her. You're human. She likes that.

However, don't turn your personal horror story into the introduction to a little lesson. When children hit this magic age, they become extremely self-centered. Your thirteen-year-old believes that whatever you're saying is strictly for her benefit or for her torture. So when parents do talk about themselves, children are quick to assume it's for the purpose of delivering a lecture with a moral point. And it's often tempting to deliver a lecture. Over dinner, Mom says to Dad, "How was your day, dear?" Dad says, "Well, my boss was giving me a really hard time and I got my back up and . . ." He goes on to describe a difficult incident at work. Then Mom says, "Okay, kids, here's an important lesson to learn from Dad's experience today . . ." And the kids say, "Can we be excused, please?" Resist the temptation to moralize.

Do reveal your feelings sometimes, about matters other than what your child is doing.

I was walking on the beach one summer day with my son, then about eleven, and out of the blue I said, "Hey, how am I doing as a parent?" He replied, "Well, there's a problem, Dad. The problem is that you're perfect, you never make mistakes." That startling exchange made me realize that I never allowed him to see me in anything like a vulnerable state. The lesson was emphasized a short while later, when our dog—who had been my dog—died at age twelve. As the dog was dying, I held him and cried. My son, witnessing this display of emotion, had a strange, upset look on his face *(what is going on here?)*. It occurred to me that in my attempts to protect my child from all pain in the world, he'd never seen me "less than perfect." He'd never seen me cry, although I had on a number of occasions. I hadn't equipped him to deal with that.

Expect, often, to feel like a fool.

This is the lot of the parent of a teenager. Adolescents today are in some ways light-years ahead of their parents. Acknowledge occasionally that there is much you don't know and suggest that you're willing to be educated. Ask your child to teach you something.

The mother of fourteen-year-old Polly was unhappy about the fact that her child was at the computer every evening, sometimes for several hours. She had no particular reasons to worry that Polly was up to something dangerous or distasteful online; she just felt increasingly distant from her daughter and her daughter's interests. So one evening she said, "I don't understand how this instant messaging works or how you Google something. Would you tell me about that? You know me, I'm kind of a technological idiot, but I'd like to learn a little more." As it turned out, Polly was pleased to give her mother a computer lesson.

Most adolescents assume that their parents don't know

what's going on in the world and are not bothered by their own ignorance. Being educable—letting your child teach you a few things—gives your teen an opportunity to communicate with you as well as a chance to be better than you. Then you need to acknowledge her relative superiority and her willingness to help you learn something.

At the same time, by virtue of your age, education, and experience, you might know that your teen's point of view concerning the stock market, third world development, or the ozone layer is somewhat misinformed or naive. Don't pull rank. Especially during the middle years of adolescence, children have opinions about issues in the world and like hearing themselves voice them. Respect and accept your child's feelings and ideas as his own and debate their fine points.

Expressing opinions, especially those he suspects are different from yours, is one way your child is trying things on for size, underscoring his existence and developing his identity. Remember that part of his goal during these years is to define himself as someone other than you.

You will not know everyone your child knows.

This comes as a shock, after all those years of arranging playdates and sleepovers, and being up on the names of every kid in your child's life. Welcome your teen's friends but don't expect to meet them all. Especially when a child reaches the middle years of adolescence, there'll be peers in her life you'll probably never hear about.

Teenagers usually don't mind having parents around, as long as Mom and Dad remain a quiet background presence. You can, of course, try to draw your child's friend into a conversation, but at some peril. Fifteen-year-old Ethan had many friends and they often congregated in Ethan's house. His friends all seemed to like his mother. "I guess that's okay," Ethan said. "Well, actually, I sort of hate it. I don't want her talking to these guys." One day his mother, a smart parent, mentioned to Ethan that she'd noticed he looked sort of annoyed and angry when she was among his friends and asked if it was all right if she spoke to them. He said, "Not too much."

Once in a while, children let down spontaneously and allow themselves to have a good time with their friends *and* their parents in the same territory, as long as it's not socially stigmatizing. If such a moment occurs, be careful. A generally low profile is safest. When they're all talking about the concert they went to and what a dumb band it was, you don't want to say, "Really, Sally? That's not what you told me when you got home. You said you really liked the band."

You can monitor your teen's activities—which means, knowing generally what she's planning for the evening and whom she'll be with and what time frame you're talking about. Adolescents don't mind this; in fact, it makes them feel safer than if you express no interest at all in what they're doing. You should not, however, banish your child's friends, and you *cannot* forbid her to see them. It won't work. If you're concerned about the types of children your teenager is spending time with, criticizing those friends or restricting her involvement with them will probably only increase their appeal in her eyes. In later chapters, I look at more effective ways to express your concerns.

Your power to shape your child's temperament is waning.

Especially as your child's personality is evolving throughout these years, it may or may not be a particularly good match with your own. If you happen to be an assertive parent of an unassertive teen, you may be tempted to push ("Oh, just go do it"). Earlier, he might have accepted a little pushing; now he resists. The better approach, one that will keep you connected, is to strategize a little, perhaps by starting out a suggestion with, "I know this kind of thing is difficult for you, but why don't you try. . . ."

I mentioned in the previous chapter the futility, and sometimes the fallacy, of labeling your child as being of one "type" or another. You can, however, appreciate the unique aspects of his personality and style, and consider if or how you might be able to smooth his path a little. During the preteen or very early teen years, when you still have some influence over your child's activities, you may see ways to shore him up, to increase his repertoire of behaviors. For example, an unassertive child might benefit from tae kwon do classes—not so that he develops the ability to punch the lights out of someone who might start harassing him or trying to lure him into unsavory activities, but so that he enjoys the feeling of having several responses to choose from in social situations.

When I was a preteen, my mother started me on piano lessons, at which I was absolutely terrible. To put me out of my misery and herself out of hers, she suggested I quit the piano and take acting lessons at a local drama school. It turned out to be one of her best ideas, because those classes taught me how to play the role of somebody other than myself. I picked up useful skills. I could go to a party and *act* like someone who was a bit more confident than I felt in reality. Later, I figured out that my mom sent me to drama school at least partly because she was socially timid herself and thought I might be able to have an easier time of it.

By watching and listening, you may spot similar ways to ease your child's passage into adolescence. Observe how he interacts with his friends. Be conscious when you're with him in public circumstances. Don't notice just how he's treating you but also how he is with other people. If you still are dropping your eleven-year-old off at school in the morning, does the crowd part and run for cover when he appears, or do other children approach him with a smile? Try to gauge the lay of the land and how your child fits in.

By such information-gathering tactics, you can keep in touch with how your young teen is changing and developing, and how you might help the process.

You cannot make your child happy.

This is the dagger to the heart of the Stage 2 parent: Your teen arrives home from school looking clearly hurt or miserable, and she won't tell you what happened. Once, when she was younger, you could give her a hug, read a story, watch cartoons together, soothe her pain. Now, often, you just have to be miserable right along with her, accepting that many of the issues she's struggling with she wants—and needs—to handle herself.

However, it is in your power to think ahead a little and anticipate when your child might be facing a particularly stressful period.

Problems of self-image and low self-esteem tend to be greatest during the early adolescent years, eleven to fourteen. Children then are highly self-conscious and suspect that everybody's looking at and evaluating them. Typically, this is also the stretch of time when your child is making the move into middle school or junior high, *and* confronting privately the scary, exciting changes that puberty brings.

That's a lot of stressors to deal with. In many ways, your child will have to struggle through them on her own. But if other external pressures are coming into play—you're moving to a new community, say—give her a little extra support. Maybe you can take some time off from work to help her get acclimated to the new surroundings, or check out a religious institution or community organization she might become interested in, or go shopping for clothes. Children can feel very alone when they're weighed down by many changes happening at once.

Some parents might reasonably anticipate that a child will face special difficulties during the teen years because of a distinguishing feature or quality that isn't going to fit the accepted norm. Consider how your child is different from the general peer group he's in. Then think about whether you might address with him some of these issues ahead of time.

Melanie had undergone reconstructive plastic surgery on her face because of a childhood accident. The only remaining evidence was a slight scar running under one side of her jaw. Her parents had emphasized all along how pretty Melanie was and assured her nobody could even see the mark on her face. Then Melanie started middle school, and classmates immediately made comments about the scar or sort of stared at it, and Melanie went into a decline—sometimes frenziedly trying to restyle her hair and arrange scarves that would hide her "deformity," sometimes spending long afternoons alone in her room with the door closed.

Mario studied studio art with a private instructor and seemed to have real talent as a painter. His parents encouraged him and placed little importance in the fact that the high school he'd be attending was noted for its outstanding sports teams and programs. It turned out that all the most popular boys were jocks; nobody was into art. Mario felt isolated and a little weird.

These loving parents only wanted to do right by their children. But what might have helped more would have been a shift into Stage 2 parenting, in which Mom and Dad asked themselves, "What's unique about our child? And how does that bode for his comfort over these years that are coming up?

Maybe we need to talk it over together with our child, before he moves into this tremendously self-conscious and social period of life."

Children become resentful when they feel that their parents have misled them: A child is assured she's so cute that nobody will notice the one thing that's not cute about her; a boy is told he's an outstanding artist and everybody loves an artist. If in the peer group that child gets raked over the coals, there can be a real feeling of betrayal *(My parents told me I was wonderful, they lied to me)*. A child who stands apart from the crowd in ways that are not generally admired can become secretive and remote about painful episodes that occur in or after school. She's suffering, she's dealing with it as best she can, and she doesn't want to talk about it to Mom or Dad, when talking about it actually might help.

A frank conversation with your child that acknowledges and enhances his identity can be important and genuinely supportive: "Let's talk about your strengths and weaknesses. You're about to go off to junior high, that's a big thing for you. What do you think you can bring to it? What are you concerned about? Do you have any worries about how other kids are going to react?"

From our adult perspective, we know that someday it will be a source of pride and a pleasure to be a fine artist, to be special in that way. But it isn't necessarily a *good* special in seventh grade, especially if it means having to devote many afterschool hours to developing that skill. In seventh grade (and for a number of years after that), your child wants, more than anything, to be visible to and accepted by his peers. They're the ones who validate his very existence. So he's worried over the things that make him different—he's not athletic, he's taller, he's fatter, he has the wrong kind of sneakers.

We assume that if one thing is going right for a child,

everything will be going right: If my son is a great swimmer, or has a wonderful voice, or is an outstanding student, all will run smoothly for him because of that. In fact, life underscores our deficiencies much more readily than it rewards our strengths. And that's especially true during adolescence.

You cannot be too visible . . . even when you're there.

My son, about eleven at the time, said to me one day, "Dad, how come you're never home when I get back from school?" I pointed out that I had a job, as he knew, and so I was not at home because I was at my job. Later, I began to think: As a university teacher, I did have some leeway in structuring my days. After discussions with my department head, I was able to rearrange my schedule so I was home two afternoons a week. Proudly, I showed up on that first afternoon, right on the spot when my son arrived back from school. "Well, what do you want to do?" I asked. Here was the rest of our conversation:

Son: "What do you mean, *do*? I'm going to start on my homework."

Dad: "Oh, okay. Would you like me to help?"

Son: "Nope."

Son, later: "I think I'll watch some TV."

Dad: "Great, what are we going to watch?"

Son: "What do you mean, *we?*"

Dad: "Do you want me to watch TV with you?"

Son: "Nope."

After another couple of my attempts at togetherness, ending with me pointing out that he had in fact expressed a wish that I were home in the afternoon, my son explained, "Gee, Dad, I don't want to be *with* you, it's just that I wanted you to be here."

It is confusing to a parent when a child says, "Be here, but don't let me know you are." Developmentally, it's important for a preteen and teen to know that Mom or Dad is sometimes in the house. But this doesn't mean that, unlike when he was younger, he actually wants to *see* Mom or Dad.

Parents often feel guilty about not being home a lot, so when they are there, they press to make it up, as I did with my son (*I'm here only two afternoons a week, I gotta get my licks in*). That easily can antagonize your child, who'll let you know in one way or another that you are to back off and give him some privacy. Don't take it personally. Parenting at this stage requires you to be a little thick-skinned. See your child's wish for you to be invisible for its developmental significance: He needs someone who cares about him in the house, just as a kind of psychological safety net; like buying insurance, he may never use it.

Interestingly, in several surveys, adolescents have ranked loneliness at the top of their list of troubles; they report they wish they had more time with their parents. Often, they say they'd like their parents simply to be around more but not necessarily interacting with them.

Don't be scarce. There's a lot to be said for simply being available, without being too noticeable and certainly without prying. In fact, that's probably the key factor in the art of parenting during this stage. Your child is comforted; also, sometimes you learn things you might want to know. Strategic placement—as when you chauffeur your child and her friends to the school dance or a sporting event or a movie—enables you to occupy an excellent inside intelligence position.

Sometimes, you might like your other child better.

One father described taking his fourteen-year-old son to a baseball game. Just the two of them, father and son. They had great seats at the park, the game was exciting—but the son had something else on his mind. He was desperate to get to a sporting goods store, about a forty-five-minute drive from the stadium, to buy some hockey equipment his father had promised him. While this dad watched the action on the field, what he heard was, "Can't we go now? Let's go, Dad. Let's go to the store. Now, okay, Dad?" His father was saying, "Hey, let's watch the game. This is a great game." But thinking all the while, *Last time I'm taking you to a game, buddy.*

A week later this father took his daughter, age nine, to another baseball game. This is what he heard from her: "Oh, I just love being with you, Daddy. Can I have another hot dog, please? Oh, I love getting a hot dog at a ball game. This is such a great game! This is so much fun!" And he was thinking, *Now there's a kid you can be a parent to.*

When you're in Stage 2 parenting, trying to alter some of your old, traditional ways of relating to your child can be especially difficult when you have children straddling that age— the oldest child crosses over while the second one isn't there yet. Here's something that can happen: You start to like your younger child better.

Some children simply do a better job than others at reinforcing their parents, or making their parents feel good about themselves. And it's often the case that a younger child is doing a better job at the moment. If you're living with one adolescent and one not-yet adolescent, you might find it a whole lot pleasanter, not to mention easier, to be with the relative youngster in the family.

What do you say when your teen—who's just told you how grossly unfair it is that you won't do something with him (which he probably didn't want you to do anyway)—accuses you of liking his kid brother or sister better than you like him?

My first recommendation: Maintain your sense of humor ("We'll get around to everything in due time, kiddo, and I'm looking at you and liking you a whole lot"). Inherently, this is the stuff of which sitcoms are made. This is what *The Wonder Years* was about. This is what *Ozzie and Harriet* was about, raising the boys. You'll laugh at it later; try to laugh a little now. Laughing at yourself a little is always to the good, which doesn't mean that a thing isn't important. Matters surrounding living with teenagers can be important and warrant your attention, but you can still treat them lightly or in a positive way.

You may develop a tin ear regarding how you sound to your child.

Here's one of the challenges of Stage 2 parenting: Occasionally, listen to yourself talking to your child. Try to hear yourself as your adolescent is hearing you. That's something parents rarely attempt, and it's a useful exercise; you can't *always* stop sounding somewhat silly to a fifteen-year-old, but maybe you'll recognize small adjustments in the way you talk that will allow your child to hear you better.

Two teenagers, juniors in high school, described a recent experience that brought them into contact with a small group of parents. Talented musicians, these boys were part of a jazz quintet that played in a private home, part of an effort to raise funds for a trip their school orchestra leader was organizing. At the end of their performance, the parents gathered around, praising their talents and making what sounded to the grown-ups like appropriate expressions of interest and enthusiasm. The teenagers thought they sounded goofy. Recounting the evening later, they mimicked their elders, no doubt with some embroidery of the words:

" 'Ooh, where did you buy such a beautiful clarinet?' asks this one lady," said one of the teens in a fake falsetto voice.

" 'I just think it's so amazing that you play so incredibly well and you're so incredibly young,' " the other teen imitated. " 'Do you have to practice every single day?' "

" 'Are you going to be a professional musician when you grow up?' "

They went on with some further examples, rolling their eyes. None of this seemed aversive to the teenagers, just a little embarrassing. Mainly they saw the adults as kind of silly and out of touch with the real world.

If you can, sometimes when you talk to your child, try to listen to yourself as if you're an adolescent too. Can you hear what might be a real turnoff to a sixteen-year-old?

You can't make your child believe what you believe.

That doesn't mean, however, that you should not convey the values you hold as the head of a family.

Many parents have belief systems and values that involve religious convictions, the importance of certain pursuits over others, or the kinds of behaviors they feel are part of becoming a worthwhile individual and a good citizen. If certain beliefs or values are important to you, do absolutely convey them to your child. Push hard on your religious values, if you have them. That's who you are, and that's the kind of family you live in.

A problem can develop, however, if you expect everyone to have the same values, including your child. Be aware that your teen may respond to your value system in several ways, depending on his developmental stage, his peer group, and, especially, how it's conveyed to him.

Here's an example. You might say, "This is what we believe, and we believe it strongly, and you might want to think about these ideas, because sometimes they're really helpful." In a sense, you are throwing out an ideological life preserver for your child to use if she really wants to use it. And she might be happy and grateful to use it, and be able to say, for example, "In my family, we believe that it's not right to have sex outside of marriage, and so I can remain a virgin and I can tell other kids that's my belief." For this child, a family belief system is comforting and helpful.

Or you might say, "This is what we believe in our family, and so this is what you believe, and consequently there are some things you cannot do." That's setting your child up to say, "Oh, yeah? You're so rigid, Mom and Dad, and I'm not like you, and you're certainly not going to make me go to church or tell me what I'm going to do with my own body."

Part of the parent's role is to throw out life preservers, and the more, the better. But you cannot force one on an adolescent. Tie the life preserver on with rope, and he'll struggle to free himself.

Parents tend to see interactions with adolescents as complete transactions, with beginnings, middles, and ends, and a nice moral to frame the story. At the end of which, our child says, "I got it, Mom, that's really great." Life doesn't proceed that way. Often, we have snippets of time in which to make ourselves heard and many partial start-and-stop conversations with an adolescent who maybe just wants to be left alone—and who's certainly not going to say, "Thanks, Mom."

In this chapter, I've suggested some ways you might make yourself a sort of caring, tuned-in presence in your preteen's and teenager's life—often in the background, always recognizing the limits of your power. In the next chapter, I look at some of those snippets of time and how to talk teen.

CHAPTER 3

Beginning the Conversation

How to Talk Teen

Ask your teen a question about his life, and he'll hear it as you lecturing, cornering, harassing, punishing, disrespecting, abusing, grilling, prying, seeking vicarious enjoyment, comparing him unfavorably to every other kid in the world, or freaking out. And that's just from, "How was school today, honey?"

Most adolescents experience personal questions from their parents as an attack of some sort. Many adolescents view much of *any* kind of talk coming from their parents with suspicion. This is one of the significant shifts occurring in your child's mind during this transitional stage.

Younger children are more directly behavioral in their responses; they're not double-guessing and analyzing the *real* (they think) meaning behind a parent's every comment. When you said to your eight-year-old, "Clean up your room now," your child's thought process, if he experienced one at all, was, *I better clean up my room or I'll get in trouble.* Say the same thing to him at fourteen, and he's thinking, *Why does she want me to clean up my room? Whose room is it, anyway? Why is she trying to control me? Nah, she's not going to get me doing that. She thinks this is messy? Hah! She ain't seen nothin' yet.* When you asked your eight-year-old how school went, he replied something like, "It was okay, we have a spelling test tomorrow." Ask your teen, and he thinks, *She's trying to get the goods on me.*

During the early adolescent years, your child becomes highly sensitized to parental communications, including those that you intend to be simple passing observations, expressions of affectionate interest, or mild requests. But these years, of course, are also just when you feel especially eager to maintain connection and get information. Because as a parent, you're also viewing your child with suspicion—in the form of worry or concern. Your daughter is acting moody, looking glum, and spending a lot of time lying on her bed staring at the wallpaper. You want to know what's wrong, or if anything is. But ask, "Is everything okay? Are you feeling sad or something?" and chances are you won't hear any news that really clues you in. You may get no response at all. You may get, "I'm fine." You may get, "Leave me alone, do you mind?" Or the obligatory adolescent eye roll or shrug.

Identifying what your child is actually hearing from you is a big part of the challenge in Stage 2 parenting. You might think you're starting a conversation in a polite, civilized, caring manner, but that's not how it seems to him. You may indeed have a hidden agenda (which, of course, your teen is probably aware of): *I don't want her spending so much time with her boyfriend. I don't want him drinking beer at the party. I want to know where she's hanging out after school.* There's nothing wrong with having a hidden agenda, but typically it's not introduced in a way that engenders anything but contempt from your child. Instead of Mom or Dad saying, "I'm concerned about something . . . ," Mom or Dad says, in effect, "Tell me what you're doing and feeling, and then I'll tell you whether or not I'm concerned about it (and I may use it against you later)."

To a child, that doesn't seem fair. It feels like a parent wielding power and taking advantage.

When I was growing up, I sometimes worked for my uncle as a cashier in his restaurant. If my cash register came up short at the end of the day, my uncle had me make up the difference out of my own pocket. If my register was over at the end of the day, I didn't get to keep the extra money. That's how your child feels, stuck in a lose-lose situation. If he could explain this to you, he might say, "You ask me about what I'm doing, and if you don't like what I tell you, I'm in trouble for it and you get on my case, but if you do like what I tell you, I don't get any appreciation for it. Or you say that's just what you expected from me, anyway. So why should I tell you anything?"

At the same time, how do you say to your teen, "I'm concerned about something . . . ," without her hearing, "I don't think you can take care of yourself" or "I don't trust you" or "I just bet you're going to lie to me?"

In this chapter, I present some ways to learn what you want (or need) to learn about your child's life at the moment, without invading his privacy or losing his trust. In the process, you promote further communication across the board—partly by acknowledging when your child is getting something right and giving a little credit where credit is due. I look at some when, where, and—especially—how possibilities for beginning the conversation.

One thread that runs through the suggestions I offer is this: Be patient. All in good time. We parents are pretty clever; we'll get around to making our point, whatever it may be, sooner or later.

When to Talk

Don't wait for a full-blown crisis.

It's an excellent idea to say to your child once in a while, "I want to have a conversation with you. Nothing's wrong. No problems. It's just that you're almost a teenager now, and I'd like to talk about some stuff."

Be prepared for your child to say, "What, are you crazy?"

Reply: "Just indulge me."

This might be the time you lay out some general rules about curfews and whatnot (more about this in a later chapter). Your teen may receive this news well. Or you may be greeted with smirking, glaring, eye-rolling, deep sighs—all those adolescent reactions that parents find annoying and infuriating. Those reactions are *meant* to be annoying; they're another way your child is staking out his identity as someone other than you. Don't be deterred or upset by them.

Actually, sighs, eye-rolling, and so on are wonderful stuff. They mean your child is listening and is hearing what you're saying. Which is what you want. Agreement with you isn't necessarily the goal.

Cool down.

If you are in the middle of a full-blown crisis, however—perhaps because an agreed-upon rule was ignored by your child or maybe the rule wasn't laid out in the first place and now you realize there's got to be one—take a little time before you get into it. Setting a rule ("You cannot ride with more than four people in the car!") or issuing a consequence ("You're grounded for a month!") at the moment of trouble usually backfires in one way or another. Say, "Let's talk about this tomorrow, when everybody's calmed down."

Where to Talk

Family meetings are fine.

Family meetings can be a great idea, although they have a terrible reputation. It all sounds very serious and formal and like anything but what a kid might want to sit through. Typically, also, they're convened when something bad has happened or might happen. To an adolescent, it's like calling her by her first and middle name—Amanda Jane! (*Uh-oh*, she's thinking, *here it comes.*)

I think the best "family meetings" happen over dinner. Turn off the TV, just sit at the table together. Chat a little about this and that. Be prepared for the fact that three out of four evenings your kids might be drumming their fingers, staring out the window, looking at the clock, and saying every five minutes, "Can I go now?"

Parenting is not a lovefest all the time; our children are not going to be especially gratifying (much less grateful) to us. But sitting around the table chatting may very well work in terms of strengthening connections and opening up communication—even though it doesn't seem to be working very much at all during these years. My children, now in their early twenties, have sometimes mentioned how much they appreciated those family dinners. Didn't seem so at the time!

Leave the house.

On the other hand, conversation sometimes happens spontaneously, revealingly, or pleasantly in some place other than home, where your usual associations are. Nobody's distracted by the TV, friends calling on the phone, or other familiar noise. Also, being somewhere else changes the mindset a bit. Turn off the cell phones, including yours.

Vacations are a good time to have these conversations, which might sound counterintuitive (vacations are supposed to be for having fun, after all). One mother was planning a week's camping trip with her husband and two sons, ages twelve and fourteen. I mentioned that she might find a way during the trip to bring up some concerns she had about the boys' friends. Her response was, "Oh, I really don't want to jeopardize this time together." But when it comes to teens, your time together is already jeopardized; you're in a rear-guard action to start with.

Vacations are good. So is a visit to a special restaurant or other spot your child likes, a place with some rewarding or fun aspect to it. But don't plan an excursion in such a way that your child owes you something. Don't take your eleven-year-old to the amusement park and say, "Now wait a minute, dear, don't run off to those rides, stay here and talk to me."

You might also suggest to your teenager occasionally, "Let's do something together as a family on Saturday morning" or "Why don't you and I go out after school today and do some shopping at the mall?" This lets your teen know that everything you do or say isn't conditional on her behavior (if she's been good, she gets a reward; if she's been bad, it's time for a talk). These casual outings offer you little oases of good communication, even if you're not talking about anything much in particular. They also give you markers to call up at some future date, when things maybe are not going so well for her or between the two of you. Then you can say, "Remember when we used to go and browse around in the mall for a while? I really miss that. I'd like to do that again."

Seize the unexpected moment.

Valerie's mom knew that something was up with her twelve-year-old daughter. Valerie often looked upset when she got back from school; there hadn't been the usual phone calls in the evening with her friends over the past week. When she asked, "Val, is something bothering you? Are you happy in school?" her daughter said, "No" and "Sure." Mom gave it up. One late evening she went into Valerie's room to put some clothes away, thinking she was asleep. She wasn't. Valerie said, "Mom, Chrissie [her best friend] dumped me. She's sitting with these other girls at lunch, and if I sit at the same table nobody talks to me." Mother and daughter discussed the situation briefly, which was all Valerie felt like doing.

Eric's father discovered that the best talks he managed to have with his son happened out of the blue when he was driving him to one or another of his after-school events. "I think it's the fact that we don't have to make eye contact," he said. "We're both looking ahead out the window, and we've got some music going on the tape player. He doesn't feel the spotlight is on him, maybe."

These can be great opening-up moments—at night right before sleep or while driving somewhere. Maybe doing the dishes, folding laundry, or putting away groceries together, or washing the car on a Sunday afternoon. There's some sense in a child's mind that it's safe now; the focus is not on her, everybody's defenses are down a little, and maybe she can slip in some news.

Many parents discover that playing chauffeur to a child and his friends can be revealing in terms of gleaning bits of information from the conversation going on in the backseat. A couple of rules: Don't look in the rearview mirror to catch your child's eye. Don't say, "What?" Don't turn around. Just mind your own business and perk up your ears. Sometimes a child sort of wants you to hear what she's letting drop. Sometimes not. Adolescent narcissism allows a child to forget that you're there in the car at all. Your child would much rather talk to her friend about some juicy topic than to notice whether or not you're listening. If you don't *look* like you're paying attention, she assumes you're not—because teens figure you're not paying much attention in general, except when they're doing something bad.

How to Talk

Here are some general suggestions that are useful when talking with your child. They are designed to get a conversation going, to prevent a conversation from stopping dead in its tracks, and to increase the odds that your child will actually hear you.

Drop a secret of your own.

Should parents have secrets from their kids? Of course. We already do. That's normal and fine. But a great parenting tool is revealing a secret of your own, from way back when.

The mother who thinks her sixteen-year-old daughter is secretly getting involved with a twenty-five-year-old man might say, "You know, I never really told anybody this, but when I was your age I went out with a thirty-year-old guy for a while. It didn't last very long, only a few dates. But I never let on to my mom or anybody. Actually, I didn't even know who I could talk to about it if I wanted to."

That's it. Mom says nothing more. But talk about getting a child's attention!

Don't sound like you're fishing for something.

Fourteen-year-old Jessica was suddenly intensely interested in boys, about whom she didn't want to say anything to her mother. One day, while she was driving Jessica to the mall, Mom said, "Something reminded me of this recently. When I was around your age, we used to rent a house at the shore for a month every summer. Well, right behind our house was another house, with an outdoor shower in a kind of wooden stall. You could see this out the window of my bedroom. The boy who lived there—I guess he was about fifteen—would take a shower out there every day when he came back from the beach, and dry himself off. I used to hide behind the blinds in my room and watch him. I felt so sneaky and guilty. One day my mom walked in and said, 'Why are you always lurking in your room in the afternoon with the blinds drawn, what are you doing?' I was mortified."

Jessica snickered and said nothing. The next day she revealed, for the first time, that there was a cute boy named Kevin in her class.

It would have been perfectly all right if Jessica hadn't let on about her crush on Kevin. That's not the point. One payoff here is that dropping a secret of your own suggests that maybe you won't recoil in horror if your child does dare to tell you something about her private life. Adolescents say to me all the time, "I can't tell my parents, they're going to freak when they hear this." Seventy-five percent of the time, they're right. When parents *don't* freak but actually take some bit of information pretty well, teenagers are pleased. They're encouraged to share a little more. So don't press.

Flash back on your own life.

What were you like at the point in your life your child is at now? Think about it. The remembrance may be startling. When our daughter, age sixteen, was seeing a boy, my wife said one day, "Don't you think she's spending too much time with this boyfriend? What do they do, do you think?" I said, "Well, she's sixteen. What were you doing with *your* boyfriend when you were sixteen?" Long pause. Wife: "Oh, God!"

But the thing is, before you can have any kind of talk with your adolescent that she might actually hear, you must try to empathize and "get in your child's head." Put yourself back there at age thirteen or sixteen. Remember how it felt. What embarrassed or scared you? What did your parents say or do that you really hated? Then you might find a useful way to talk about your experiences when you were in the position your child might be in now, or if your child may be facing some of the same situations. Remembering yourself back when, you'll be less likely to start off with, "Let me tell you something . . ." or "When you get to be my age . . ." Actually, getting to be your age is a good thing. If the memories of your sixteen-year-old self are unsettling, it's also reassuring to know that you turned out fairly well anyway, and so will your child.

Listen first, speak second.

It's the hardest thing for parents moving into Stage 2 parenting: Listen first, then talk. You can always talk, but speaking first has a powerful tendency to stop all conversation cold. Listen to what your child is saying, then contribute according to what you've just heard.

After you've listened and you feel you have something pertinent or necessary or appropriate to say, notice what happens after you make your opening comments. I don't have a lot of sure-fire scripts to offer—first say this, then say that—because all good communication is interactive. You need to be alert to and aware of how your child is responding to what you're doing. Does he say, "I don't want to talk about this anymore"?

Or does he sound suddenly angry? Intense emotion is significant—usually, it means that you're on to something, or this subject is an issue for him.

Suppose you've asked your child, mildly, "How was the party?" Then you've listened to what he wants to tell you. Then, still mildly, you ask, "Was there drinking going on?" And your child replies, snappishly, "Nooo!?" (in that sort of drawn-out syllable with a rising inflection at the end, suggesting you must be insane even to think such a thing). There's at least a fifty-fifty chance that your teen had some beer and knows you're not going to like it. If he hadn't had some beer, his reply might be something like, "Nah, I don't think there was a lot of drinking." The transcript may look the same, but the emotion is different. Listen for the emotion. It may tell you a lot.

Listening first—or listening longer—may also cause you to change your mind about what you'll say. In a situation in which you feel you should act immediately, be firm, and assess appropriate consequences for some behavior, still take the time to hear your child out. Adolescents often complain, "My dad grounded me for a month and he didn't even listen to the whole story. There was nothing I could say. If he'd listened to the whole story and then grounded me, I wouldn't have liked it, but I'd have understood." Those are the teens who start thinking the next time, *Okay, I'm not going to tell you what happened, Dad, because you're just going to ground me for life anyway, so why should I bother?*

Sometimes it's useful to write down what your child said, privately and after the conversation the two of you had—especially if you were concentrating hard on hearing her out and at the same time holding back on some comments of your own that you sensed would not open up the communication. At a later, calmer moment, you'll probably be able to consider what she was telling you from a more objective point of view.

Create a space for your child to step into.

The opposite of creating a space for your child to step into is saying, "Here's how it is, my way or the highway, don't let me catch you doing that again."

Alex's father was pretty sure something serious was on his son's mind. Alex, fourteen, was unusually quiet and looking worried. His dad also thought the situation had something to do with a couple of boys Alex had been hanging out with recently. Alex's mother had learned from another mother that Ted, Alex's new pal, got a two-day suspension for showing up in school with a marijuana plant decal pasted on the sleeve of his jacket.

Alex's father suggested he and Alex drive down to the gas station to get the oil checked on the car. On the way, Dad started a conversation. "You know, I was thinking the other day about something that happened to me when I was about your age, and it's really kind of stuck with me all these years. This friend of mine, a kid named Jack, talked me into drinking his dad's liquor. We did that every afternoon for about a week. I wasn't very happy about it, but I never really knew what to do. His father finally found out, he talked to my father, and my dad hit the ceiling. He said, 'Don't ever do anything like that again, because it's stealing and it's illegal to drink at your age.' And he was right, but I wasn't exactly sure how to deal with the whole situation.

"What got me thinking about all that was, Mom heard that Ted was suspended because of some drug thing. I know you and Ted are really tight right now, so I was wondering if you're kind of in that same place I was in. Let me know if I can help, or if you'd like to talk something over."

At the time, Alex didn't immediately spill the beans and tell all. But his dad had made an opening, a space for him to step into if he wanted to talk.

Consider what's *not* being said.

And whether that actually says a lot. Turn down the volume and look at the picture instead.

Don't just take your child at his verbal word. Think, *How is he acting? Has anything changed recently? He can hardly drag himself out of bed every morning. He's picking out-of-the-blue arguments with his kid brother. He's dropped a previous passion for the guitar.* So many times a parent says, "How're you doing, son?" and son replies, "Great." But he looks dreary all the time and he seldom leaves his room. Or he says, "Great," with arms folded over his chest and a furious scowl on his face. So chances are he's not really feeling all that great.

Ask "open" questions.

Given that adolescents generally prefer not to be questioned at all, or take all questions as a parent's attempt to pry into their secret lives, it is still possible to gain more information by this useful tactic: Switch "closed" questions to "open" questions. A closed question allows a teen to escape with a one-word answer: "How was your day?" "Good." An open question virtually compels a child to offer a more detailed reply: "What happened when your coach posted the new schedule for swim practice this term?"

Ask without asking.

Asking without asking is often a good tactic—if only because asking *with* asking is received with such distaste and resentment by teenagers.

The indirect approach—coming at a particular issue that's on your mind without putting your child on the spot—can open things up. For example, the following icebreakers might be heard by the typical teenager as not too personally threatening and invasive, or not as a grilling.

Linda's mother wants to ask her child if she's unhappy about something at school. She says, "Your grades have been great, Linda. But I haven't heard you talk about school much lately. Do you still like that history teacher?"

Frank's father wants to ask his son about what he does when he goes to friends' parties. He says, "I heard you talking with David about a party he had when his parents were out of town. What happened when they got home?"

Merry's mother wants to ask Merry if she's feeling any pressures in her peer group to become sexually active. She says, "I saw in the news yesterday a story about a boy who got arrested for date rape. Did you hear that? Do you think that kid should have been arrested?"

Owen's mom wants to ask her son if there's a lot of drinking going on with boys he knows. She says, "Did you know that if a kid has a party with alcohol at his house, his parents can be arrested? And if any of the kids who've been drinking get in a car accident driving home, those same parents can be held responsible? That might be one reason why Tim's parents flipped out."

Sherry's mother wants to ask Sherry if she's developing dangerous eating habits. She says: "I've noticed you don't have much of an appetite at dinner lately. Is my cooking all right? Am I losing my touch?"

Here's how one parent led up to asking without asking. Brian, thirteen, had been pestering his mother for months to get him a particular leather jacket. Finally, for his birthday, Brian got the jacket he had lusted after. For two weeks he wore it to school every day; then one afternoon, he came home without the jacket. His mother was upset and angry but wisely refrained from sounding off to her son ("We got that jacket for

you against our better judgment, we just can't get you anything valuable anymore, you can't take care of your things,"
and so on). She asked Brian what had happened; he said he lost
the jacket. Did he know where he lost it? No.

Brian's mother had several reasons for suspecting that the
jacket had actually been stolen by one or another of the older
boys in his school. But Brian looked guilty and shamefaced; his
mom thought he believed he was just too much of a major disappointment to his parents to say what really happened. So she
tried to create a somewhat different kind of communication
with her son. A couple of days after the jacket went missing,
she said to Brian, "You know, sometimes people have things
stolen, and they know about it but they couldn't stop it from
happening. Or they didn't know what to do afterward. I just
had this thought that I wonder if somebody could have taken
your jacket."

She let Brian know she had some suspicions, but in a way
that deflected the blame from her son. Then he was buoyed up
enough to tell her that he left his jacket in the lunchroom,
remembered it after last class, raced back to get it, but it was
gone.

Be specific . . . with a willing heart.

This is sort of the reverse of asking without asking. Parents do
have questions, particular things they want to know more
about. It's appropriate to ask them, specifically. Kids don't
appreciate parents being coy. But here's one important point:
Know exactly what information you're after. Know the question you really want answered. The following bit of conversation between Kelly and her mother is an example of what I
mean.

Kelly had a curfew of eleven P.M., but she was regularly

dragging in around midnight. Her parents were concerned, because they were aware that fifteen-year-old Kelly had a new boyfriend who was several years older than she. On a couple of evenings, they asked their daughter when she walked in the door, "Hey, how come you're not getting in on time? What've you been doing?" That was an easy one for Kelly to pass off: "Oh, just hanging out, nothing much."

On another evening, her mom said, "I'm concerned about your going past your curfew all the time, why is that happening?" Kelly replied, "Oh, Mom, so what? Everybody stays out this late."

But here's what Kelly's parents *really* wanted to know and to convey to their child: "We're concerned that you're becoming sexually involved with your new boyfriend, especially because he's older, and staying out so late maybe means that you're finding yourself in compromising situations that you don't like but you can't get out of." Kelly's mother gave this conversation another try. She was empathetic enough to realize that saying something like, "You're not sleeping with this boy, are you?" would be a very bad idea. She wanted to be specific, she wanted to maintain a caring tone, and she wanted to gain further information. She said, "Kelly, it's really not the curfew that your dad and I are thinking about. We're concerned that you might be feeling pressured into having sex with your boyfriend."

Now, being appropriately specific and putting your concern out there doesn't mean a child will say, "You know, Mom, you're right. Thanks for asking and telling me what's on your mind." More than likely, the teenager will be outraged anyway. Kelly's response to her mother's expression of concern was interesting. She said, "Well, even if I am having sex, why do you care?"

Her mom was absolutely stupefied. She replied, "Of course I care. I don't want you to be hurt."

At which Kelly looked annoyed and said, "You know what I think? This is really about you wanting me to be a goody-goody, because that makes you look great. It's all about your feelings and your reputation. But I'm going to live my own life."

This was hurtful to her mom and also angered her. Back-tracking, she said, "Look, we said we want you home by eleven, and we expect you here by eleven."

Conversationwise, that was a stopper.

But this adolescent's question—why do you care?—was worth some thought on her mother's part. Why did she want to know more about this private aspect of her daughter's life? Was she afraid for her safety, that she might be raped? Was she worried that her child might contract a disease or become pregnant? Were those legitimate worries, knowing what she did about her daughter? How could she convey them?

Here's how Kelly's mother might have continued to express her concerns: "Okay, yeah, it is about me a little, I do want to feel like a good parent. But I remember that at your age some-times I was in situations I couldn't get out of, and that fright-ened me. I just want to make sure that's not going on for you. These decisions about intimacy and intimate relationships are really hard. And I think it's harder for you now than when I was your age. It seems more dangerous, people need to be really careful. Better to be safe than sorry, as they say. So I'm really asking not to pin you down or reprimand you or butt into your personal life. I just want to make sure I'm giving you whatever resources you need."

She'd be telling her daughter that the curfew existed to protect Kelly against an unpleasant event, and she really wanted to know if the event was occurring and if she could be of help. Once the conversation opened up in that way, the two might be able to talk together about how to handle whatever *was* going on. Possibly a curfew wasn't especially useful. Possibly, in her heart of hearts, Kelly was thinking, *Maybe I better stick to this curfew, because what happens in that last hour is that we always end up going to my boyfriend's friend's house, and there's a lot of out-of-control people there and I actually am a little scared.*

Here's where the open heart comes in. Suspend judgment. That's not to say your child's behavior should be perfectly okay with you. But we catch more flies with honey than with vinegar, and your goal should be to promote communication. If the situation is one that warrants setting a limit, then a limit should be set, briefly. But in many cases, setting a limit—your curfew is eleven—is when communication stops. There's nothing interactive when a parent says, as she has the power to do, "You're not getting home on time. That's it, you can't go out anymore."

Write a letter.

By all means, write a letter or a note and leave it on your child's desk (as long as you're certain it won't be found by an independent party) or send an e-mail, if there's something you want to say and, for whatever reason, it's difficult to voice. These are all ways of attempting to communicate; relying solely on "having a talk" makes it easy to become defeated or never to find the snippet of time in which to do so.

Some children themselves might find it easier or more comfortable to communicate thoughts or a piece of news to parents by writing a note.

When I was in sixth grade, my father gave me a watch, my first *good* watch, and spoke to me about what a serious responsibility this was; I needed to take care of that good watch. Four weeks later, playing in the gym, I lost it. I was mortified, horrified, wondered how I could tell my dad or even if I should tell him at all. For a week, I was a wreck—wearing long-sleeved shirts so my father wouldn't notice the missing watch, alluding to my watch as if it was still there ("Oh, I must have left my watch upstairs"). Finally, after confessing all to my mother and getting her thoughts on the matter, I decided I would write my dad a letter, since I was simply too upset to face him. The letter was poignant, self-deprecating, soul bearing: "Dad, I have some news to tell you that I know will disappoint you . . . I realize there are some things in life that can never be forgiven, some mistakes can never be undone . . . I am going to live the rest of my life to prove to you that I am a responsible person . . ."

My mother gave the letter to my father; I asked my mother what his response had been. "Well," she said, "he read it very carefully. . . . No, he didn't say anything. . . . No, his face didn't get red. . . ." He never did speak to me about the lost watch, and I can only assume my father believed from my confession that I'd suffered enough and the less said the better.

It was not like me to write, but I felt relieved. Writing a letter created a bit of safety, a bit of distance; it enabled me to express an event and the feelings that went with it in a way that left me feeling in control of a difficult moment. You or your child may find various ways of breaking down the barrier that sometimes makes beginning the conversation hard. Put a yellow sticker on the dashboard of your teen's car: "I'm angry, but I'll get over it. Love, Mom."

Maintain a supportive tone.

Asking for information with a supportive tone means that you're not necessarily condoning what your child has done, but you're going to try to understand why she did it. You must believe that your child is good and that she's doing the best she can—just as you're doing the best you can. This mind-set is conveyed in the way you talk to her, in your tone.

Tone has to do usually with how you phrase things. For example, there's the accusing tone, which suggests Mom or Dad is pretty sure the child is being deceitful—"Did you *really* go over to Sarah's house to do homework this afternoon?" There's the tone that implies disappointment—"You didn't forget to put gas in the car again, did you?" There's the fearful tone, suggesting catastrophe—"I couldn't get to sleep, I was so afraid you were in an accident when you didn't get home on time!"

These forms of opening a conversation are likely to make the teen even more evasive in the future about where she goes in the afternoon, or how come she didn't get gas, or why she was out late.

A supportive tone in these situations might sound like this:

Say: "Well, good, I guess that means you won't have so much homework over the weekend. Maybe you and I can do a little shopping."

Say: "Thanks for coming in on time, I appreciate it. I know it's hard to get gas and also be home on time. Did you put gas in the car? It's helpful for me when I go to work in the morning and I know I don't have to stop for gas."

Say: "When you're not home, I'm worried that something's happened and that makes me worry also that I haven't been a good enough parent. I'm not really dumping on you."

As teenagers, my two children got a few scratches and dings on our car over the years. Much later, they actually thanked me for the fact that I was able to say, "It's just a car, as long as you're okay," instead of, "Oh, God, what happened with the car?!" My supportive tone didn't make them rush out to scratch the car again; it did make them more likely to tell the truth about what happened.

Play it cool.

Try not to overreact, no matter how shocked you are by what you're hearing from your child. Maintain a poker face and keep listening.

One of the times a parent may find it most difficult to play it cool is when a child seems to be divulging a secret or asking for advice, but the message is disguised as "all those other guys" are doing something. Your child says, "I know this kid who was smoking pot in the park across from school and a teacher caught him." Or "Most kids think it's okay to drink at parties as long as you don't drive." Or "The school nurse says even condoms don't always keep you from getting AIDS."

Mom's or Dad's instinct is to pounce on this bit of "sharing" and say immediately, "You smoke pot?" "You were drinking at that party?" "You're having sex, aren't you?"

Try to play it cool. Your child is giving you an opening, from which you might talk generally about pot smoking, beer drinking, or the reliability of condoms. Or you might want to keep the conversation going by asking about that other guy: "Oh, did that kid get into a lot of trouble when the teacher saw him smoking?"

When your child tells you some details about a hurtful thing that's been happening to her with her friends, your tendency is to overreact. It's terribly painful to see a son or daughter going through a rough time because of teasing, ostracizing, or peer pressure of other kinds. Maybe you went through something similar, so you can imagine what your child is feeling, and you want to take the pain away. But when you respond in an over-the-top manner, with fury and dismay and excessive protectiveness, your teen thinks, *Oh, no, now Mom's going to call up Shawna's mother and tell her everything and I'm ruined.* That's horrifying to an adolescent. Playing it cool works better, which doesn't mean you come across as uncaring or unsympathetic.

It means, for one thing, being calm enough to make a plan with your child. If she's just let drop some specifics about how the popular clique in school has been making her day a long stretch of misery, maybe you can say, "Ouch. That sounds so painful. What kinds of things have you tried? How can I be of help here?" Or maybe, "You know, if I were in your position, I don't think I'd know what to do. I'm not sure I know what to do now. So let's talk about it a little, what could we consider?"

Whatever information your teen has conveyed to you, your first response should be to express appreciation for the confidence. Then, take a deep breath, count to ten, wait until tomorrow, give yourself some time to think things through before deciding whether the problem at hand is sufficiently threatening to warrant further action on your part. Often, you've filled your appropriate role already; your listening ear was all your teenager needed to vent his anxiety, fear, or anger.

After sharing his secret, he may feel back in control—and actually feel violated if you decide to act on what he's told you. Wait it out a bit to see how he handles the situation on his own. You can always step in at a later time. Your child needs to feel she has an ally, somebody who's going to listen to her. Playing it cool is one way to reinforce those feelings. Unconditional positive regard, not conditional listening (even with the best intentions), is what you want.

Don't go for the mile; be happy with the inch.

Resist the urge to get in the last word or, after achieving 50 percent compliance from a teen, to push for 60 percent. Getting in the last word can ruin a decent, productive conversation. The following three stories illustrate that point. They're also about the importance of acknowledging when a child is getting something right.

Jason had never been given a curfew by his parents. Now, at age seventeen, he'd sometimes just go away overnight, staying with one friend or another. His parents were beside themselves, but since they'd never set a curfew, they didn't know how to approach the whole thing at this relatively late date. So they brought Jason to therapy and stated up-front that they wanted him to have a curfew, he'd have to be home by midnight. Jason protested, "That's not fair. I'm pretty much grown up now, I should be able to come and go whenever I want, I'm just staying with friends," and on and on. His parents said no, it was time for Jason to have a curfew. Parents and son negotiated back and forth. And the parents expressed their concerns appropriately for the most part. They said, "Look, when you're not home at night, we're worried. We don't always know where you are. We wouldn't know how to reach you if we needed to. So we just have to know more about your whereabouts."

Finally, parents and son brokered an agreement: Jason would call at eleven if he wasn't home, and he'd tell his parents at that time when he would be home or if he was staying over with a friend. Jason agreed, grudgingly; he promised he'd call at eleven. At the very end, his father said, "Good. Now I think we should work toward your being in at midnight every day."

Jason just lost it. He said, "Weren't you listening to anything I said? Wasn't this all about my being responsible and letting you know when I'd be home, and now you just said it's not okay?" He felt manipulated and got up and walked out.

Lizzie, fourteen, didn't bathe very often. She was lax about personal hygiene, in a willful way—she wasn't lazy, she just didn't want to take showers and she wouldn't discuss the matter with her parents. Again, in therapy, the parents presented their arguments. Lizzie's mother, in particular, was rigid about the issue—at least every other day, she told her daughter, you have to shower. After a lot of further talk, Lizzie's father said, "Well, look, I can understand that you don't feel like showering, but you have to think about how other people see you. Maybe it's noticeable that you don't always look very clean, and that reflects badly on you." Lizzie: "Yeah, okay, I can understand that."

So this was ending up agreeably, with Mom, Dad, and Lizzie planning to stop on the way home to buy some new cosmetics and bath products for her to use. At the very end, Mom said, "But I have to tell you, no child of mine is going to go without bathing for two days in a row." Lizzie stormed out.

Brian, a seventh grader, did poorly in school the first term. His parents learned about his dismal performance when Brian's math teacher phoned his mother and suggested that Brian needed tutoring to pass the course.

Brian and his parents argued about his grades.

Mom: "You're very smart, basically an A student, but you're bringing home C's and even a D."

Brian: "School sucks."

Dad: "You're not studying enough. You've just got to work harder."

Brian: "I'm in seventh grade, it's no big deal. When I'm in ninth grade and I have to study, I'll study."

Eventually, Brian gave up the arguments. They made an agreement: Brian would buckle down, study more, and bring his grades up by the end of the year. And he did. His final report card had all B's.

Now, a nice response to Brian's performance might have been, "Great job. I'm glad you could clutch victory from the jaws of defeat. I know it's been tiring for you, but I knew you could do it." Here's what Brian heard instead. From his mom: "See, you could have been doing this all along." From his dad: "And you know, Brian, you're still not working up to your full potential. That's what we'd like to see next year."

His parents no doubt were right about his potential and about what he could have been doing all along. Some parents will say, "I don't want to reinforce mediocre behavior. Sure, he's improved, but somebody's got to drive him to do even better." To which I say, All in good time. A child in Brian's situation is often tremendously proud of what he's been able to accomplish. When he doesn't get credit for small gains made, when no one appreciates them, it doesn't seem fair. And he's easily discouraged. Why shouldn't Brian ease up on himself and go back to pulling C's and D's, since his parents were unimpressed by his achievements?

In fact, fostering rebellion or truly dangerous secrecy in a child may be an unintended consequence of failing to acknowledge a job well done or an accommodation made—and an unintended consequence of getting in the last word.

Quit while you're ahead.

The experiences of Jason's, Lizzie's, and Brian's parents are really about quitting while you're ahead, which is an excellent rule any time you're talking with your teen about his private life. Stick to the old show-business rule: "Always leave 'em wanting more." It's far better to solicit frequent small bits of information than to try to force long "confessions" from your child all at once. Even when he wants you to know about a problem, it's hard for him to give up his privacy. He'll manage better—and you'll have a better chance of beginning a possibly important conversation—if he's allowed to divulge his secrets at his own pace.

Quitting while you're ahead also means not belaboring things, even when they're good things. One mother had what she described as "a fantastic talk" with her fourteen-year-old daughter, as the two of them were eating ice cream and watching *Sleepless in Seattle* on TV one Friday night. The daughter told her mom about some kids in school who were getting boyfriends and how that made the other girls jealous. The mother told her daughter about some of her own experiences in high school. When the movie was over and both were feeling pleasantly tired, the girl said, "Good night, Mom, I love you."

The following day, Mom wanted to bask in the good feelings some more and reinforce the open atmosphere, and she said to her daughter, "Wasn't that a great talk we had last night? I was just thinking of something else about what we were saying . . ." Her daughter cut her off with, "Oh, God. I never should have had that stupid conversation with you in the first place." She left the house. Sometimes it's a mistake to revisit a good conversation a day later.

Just as it's a mistake to pull out a grocery list of points you want to make—"and another thing . . ."—don't expect to cover all the bases on your mind in one conversation.

Curb the need to be right.

Of course, circumstances often prove that you *were* right. The temptation is to point this out to your child, an I-told-you-so observation. We parents do that because we want our children to pay attention to what we're saying, maybe to listen better next time. But there's something else too: We'd like a little validation. You may be waiting for your teen to say, "You know, you were right, and you're right about a lot of things, Mom, and I appreciate it."

Don't hold your breath. Those are words you're not going to hear at this point in time.

Acknowledge your child—to someone else.

One of the things adolescents hate but also love is when parents brag about them a little to other people. They may cringe, they may walk away, but they do like it. The bit of bragging doesn't have to be specific. It should definitely not be remotely humiliating ("My son is so handsome, so athletic, you wouldn't believe what this boy can do!"). Just a little verbal pat on the back in front of someone else. My mother used to refer to me as "a good kid." We might meet an adult friend of hers on the street; she'd say, "This is my son Peter." The adult friend might say, "Well, hello, Peter, you're a tall fellow." My mother would say, "He's a really good kid."

That was important to her, my being a good kid. It was important to me. And it was enough said.

Parents are sometimes nervous about communicating with their teenager, oddly self-conscious with this child they used to talk to so freely and who's suddenly viewing them with something like contempt. "I'm afraid of looking and sounding like an idiot," said one mother. "My daughter—her friends, too—are all so cool and hip."

My advice is that you can't avoid looking like an idiot. You *will* look like one at times. Don't worry about it. Just speak from the heart.

I'm also, as this book shows, very much in favor of turning yourself in sometimes. Own up to your idiocy. Acknowledge that you don't have all the answers. Admit that maybe you made a mistake. In therapy or in my groups, a teen occasionally responds to some remark I've just made with, "What?

What did you say that for? Geez!" And I say, "Oh, I'm sorry, that's one of those stupid questions adults are always asking. I was just trying to figure out what was going on in your head. How can I ask that in a different way?"

I have some cover because I'm a therapist. I can say, "Sorry, that was really a shrinky remark." But parents can do the same, and in the process they do themselves and their children and the whole matter of starting the conversation a great service. When you turn yourself in, you're letting your child know you don't consider yourself infallible and you're not attempting to catch him out in something. You're letting him know you're trying to be open, honest, and caring.

That atmosphere is especially important when it comes to the issues that really get your antennae waving—boyfriends, girlfriends, sex, cigarettes, beer, peer pressure, bodily changes, and other matters that your child isn't talking to you about. In the following chapter, I consider what you do and don't need to know about all that.

CHAPTER 4

Your Teenager's Life, Right Now

What You Do and (Probably) Don't Need to Know

When my daughter was thirteen, I was driving her and two of her girlfriends to a soccer game one afternoon when I overheard the friends asking all about her new "boyfriend." This was news to me, that my daughter had a boyfriend, and I experienced the slight jolt of surprise and anxiety that most parents in this situation would feel. My impulse was to interrupt the conversation to ask, half kiddingly, "So, a boyfriend, huh? Who is this guy? When did all this start?" I kept my mouth shut, however, and just continued driving. The boyfriend event signified an important moment in her adolescent development and there was no reason for me to complicate it—maybe even spoil it somewhat—by fishing for information. I would have *liked* to hear more. But I didn't *need* to know, at least certainly not right then and there.

An adolescent's first romance is only one of the many issues bubbling up during these years that pique a parent's curiosity—or other reactions ranging from mild concern to deep worry. But it can be extremely difficult to avoid crossing the line between ordinary interest and an invasion of a child's delicate sense of privacy, even when you're referring to the most mundane events of his day. You probably think you're simply being pleasantly involved when you ask, "What movie did you guys see tonight? Any good? Did you stop for something to eat afterward?" Your spouse or a friend might feel comfortable answering such questions; your teenager is just as likely to feel resentful and respond to your expression of interest with nothing more than a glare.

On the other hand, when your child comes home from a party or an evening with friends, should you say nothing at all? Saying nothing at all isn't typically the sign of a loving, caring, interested parent, which is actually what your adolescent wants you to be.

In this chapter, I talk about several "big" issues, experiences or behaviors that probably will be part of your child's life over the teen years. Regarding some—and a few items on my list may surprise you—the better part of wisdom is to bite your tongue, refrain from quizzing your child, and assume that matters are running their course relatively normally. Clearly, this isn't always easy to put into practice. But not demanding chapter and verse about what your teenager is doing when he's out of your sight has three desirable benefits, at least.

First, your child will not feel as if you're prying, for reasons that make no sense to him. This is all to the good, because once a child perceives Mom or Dad as simply nosy and interfering, he'll usually go to even greater efforts to keep his life off-limits. In fact, I believe that a parent's intrusiveness sometimes motivates an adolescent to engage in even riskier or more parent-provoking activities.

Second, not knowing what you really don't need to know is easier on your nerves. Quite often, learning that your child has acquired some bit of "adult" awareness or has engaged in a (to you) worrisome behavior leaves you with nothing much to do about it, anyway—except feel vaguely agitated. One evening some years ago, my family and a few friends were playing a game of charades. My daughter, then about nine, was a crackerjack charades player and she and I were usually an unbeatable team. This time, my assignment was to act out the movie *Dick Tracy*, and I ran into trouble immediately. Now, if we had been an all-adult, largely male audience, the "dick" part would have been a cinch. After I failed at my charade, my daughter was extremely frustrated. She said, "Dad, you're usually so good at this, I can't believe we didn't get this one, it was so easy." "Well," I said, "I just couldn't think of how to do 'Dick.' " My daughter pointed at her crotch and said, "For pete's sake, why didn't you just go like this!?"

My first thought was: *How does she know that?* My second thought was: *Actually, I don't want to know how she knows that.*

The third benefit, and the most important one: In many cases, jumping into the middle of a situation you suspect your child is struggling with—attempting to "fix" what's going wrong or making her unhappy—prevents her from fighting her own battles, reaching her own conclusions, managing her own emotions and, essentially, growing up some more. And that's what she has to do. Much of the tough stuff she will go through you simply cannot fix and make right for her, as desperately as you might want to do so.

It helps to keep in mind that many behaviors you find disturbing or think you ought to learn more about are transient matters in your adolescent's development—rites of passage, growing pains, trial runs, and not particularly harmful. So biting your tongue is smart. Which doesn't mean saying nothing at all. It's right, obviously, to let your child know you're interested in his life—you're glad he had fun at the party, you're sorry he didn't have fun at the party, you'd be happy to hear what he thought about the movie. Teenagers make it very clear when they're not in the mood to talk, and you can take the hint (without taking it personally) and change the subject or drop the conversation, at least for the time being. But in addition, sometimes you may want to comment on your child's business because you know you have something to offer, information or perspectives she should hear. It's a proper part of your role as a parent. In those situations, it's possible to get your point across without getting your child's back up—not too much, anyway. (Later in this chapter, you'll see some helpful hints on how you might walk that tricky line.)

Finally, there are times you *do* need to know the nitty-gritty details about a teen's "secret" life. The bottom line is, you must step forward when you believe that your child's physical or emotional safety is seriously threatened. As I recommended in the previous chapter, try to lay out some ground rules for future interaction, long before any trouble is likely to arise. It's all right to say, in so many words, "Here's what I'm going to get hysterical about—STDs, alcohol, drugs, guns. If I suspect you're getting into trouble with any of that, I'm going to ask you a lot of questions and take some action because it scares me to death."

Here, now, some suggestions on what you don't need to know. A good place to begin involves exploring your own agenda.

What Do You Want to Know and Why Do You Want to Know It?

The "what" part of this question you'd probably have no difficulty answering. You want to know if your daughter is having sex with her boyfriend or if she's being ostracized by a clique at school, if everybody was drinking at the party your son went to or if he's got a collection of *Playboy* magazines somewhere in his room. Maybe you want to know:

- What does he do in the bathroom for two hours at a time?

- What is she telling her friend over the phone that clearly I'm not supposed to hear?

- What is he up to from three to six every day after school?

- Is my daughter happy?

- Does my son have nice friends?

The "why" part of the equation is more complicated. But to get a handle on all the small moments in the course of a day when you're tempted to ask your child to tell you something that he probably doesn't want to tell you, it can be useful to spend some time thinking over the "why."

- I want to help my child with a problem I'm sure he's having.

- I want to get more information, to find out if he can handle the problem on his own.

- I want to protect him.

- I want to let her understand I'm somebody she can talk to.

- I want to point my child down the right path, help him learn the behaviors that are acceptable and rewarded in our society, and I'm the best one to impart those lessons.

- I want to feel like I'm being a good parent.

- I want to experience what my child is experiencing.

- I want to know about her life, because she used to tell me everything and now she doesn't, and that makes me feel abandoned and not so important to her anymore.

- I want to know because I'm anxious about everything, and I can't stand feeling that way.

All these "why I want to know" reasons are understandable. Some are better reasons than others. Certainly, for example, we try to find out about our children's affairs partly for our own benefit, to help us feel good about ourselves and the job we're doing. There's nothing wrong with that. From my own experience as a parent of adolescents, I remember occasionally thinking, *I'm glad I asked my son/daughter about that thing going on last week. I'm not sure what I heard back was the absolute truth, or that I got the whole story. But it was right to bring up the subject and show my interest and concern because that's what a father does.*

Sometimes you do want to glean further information, so you'll have enough facts to decide whether you should butt out and leave matters up to your child or intervene with useful advice or practical help. Sometimes you want to send the message that you'll be a willing ear if she wants to talk. But adolescents are pretty smart about the "whys" behind a parent's poking around for details. For one thing, they bitterly resent it when they believe—perhaps appropriately—that a parent is seeking vicarious excitement, or wants to experience what his or her child is experiencing. One seventeen-year-old boy said this about his father: "My dad is always asking me things like if I'm having any good make-out sessions or if the kids I hang out with are 'getting it on,' as he says. This is all in a kind of guy-to-guy, joking around way. It's creepy. He's just trying to get some little fantasies going for himself. I think it pisses him off that he grew up in a really uptight family and never got a chance to fool around when he was my age."

One sixteen-year-old girl said about her mother: "I'm the last kid still at home, the baby. My parents don't have a real happy marriage. My mom asks me all these questions about my boyfriend, about my girlfriends, what clothes I'm going to pack for this overnight trip with my class. I try to be polite and tell her a few things, because it's really sort of pathetic. She doesn't have a life."

What teens object to most is the interrogation. But you can initiate a conversation, express a concern, convey information, gather a few salient facts, open the door—all without quizzing, poking, and prying. The following questions are among those most frequently on parents' minds, and they involve issues that teens typically want to keep secret. If you're stewing over some of them, that's probably a sign that your adolescent's development is proceeding on schedule and he or she is actively, appropriately stirring up a little parental anxiety. Think about your own "why I want to know" answers. Then consider these ideas on how to achieve the balance between being involved and being invasive.

What You (Probably) Don't Need to Know About Your Teen's Life, Right Now

Does my thirteen-year-old have a boyfriend/girlfriend?

Here are several relevant points: First, what you mean by a boyfriend/girlfriend isn't necessarily what your child means.

The father of a young adolescent girl had been noticing the same young adolescent boy around the house frequently and asked his daughter one Saturday afternoon if she and Josh were going on a date that evening. "A *date?*" she said, in a tone of disgust. "No, Dad, we're not going on a *date*, we're meeting a bunch of people at the diner." This father had difficulty figuring out the social scene his child was part of. "On the one hand, these kids seem to get into the boyfriend/girlfriend thing earlier than ever," he said. "In my day, you didn't have a real girlfriend until later in high school. But at the same time, nobody now seems to be actually *dating*, where the two of you have a plan and you go out somewhere. They spend their time traveling around in little packs."

That was a pretty accurate description of how adolescents typically get together. Some years ago, researchers identified the stages of a child's social development. First, they associate exclusively with same-sex friends, then they join mixed-sex groups, and finally they become part of a couple by the middle adolescent years. That progression is not so typical anymore. Children remain in the group stage a lot longer, which may or may not be a positive factor in terms of learning what goes into constructing a personal relationship. In any case, observe a group of young teens gathered at the mall, and you'll see that they're not necessarily divided equally between males and females. In random groupings, there may be a bunch of girls and a guy or two, or a bunch of guys and a girl or two. A lot of teens also talk about just "hooking up," or engaging in some sexual behavior with an individual who isn't particularly considered a boyfriend or girlfriend.

The point is, it's not always easy for a parent to know what's going on, and asking about a child's "boyfriend" may be at best unrevealing.

Here's perhaps a good way of opening the door. If you do have an inkling that your thirteen-year-old is moving into boyfriend territory, make some general statements to let her know that you're aware this kind of thing might be happening— without saying you're pretty sure it's happening with her and you're kind of anxious about that. You might say, "You know, you're getting really grown up. You're a very pretty girl, and boys are going to start approaching you, if they haven't already.

Sometimes it's hard to decide what to do or how to respond. So I just want you to know that I'm more than happy to chat with you if you have any thoughts about all this. I know things are different now from when I was your age, but I really would like to be helpful. I think that's what moms and dads are for."

When it's obvious a child does have The Boyfriend or The Girlfriend, she or he usually wants to keep this precious development a private matter. An adolescent's romance can be a wondrous, exciting, scary experience. The *end* of a romance, when a boyfriend/girlfriend breaks things off, can be a horrendous, highly emotional, upsetting experience. In either case, you don't really need to know all the details if your child clearly prefers not to let you in on them. Here are some of the lessons she's learning from her romantic involvement: how to compromise on social plans, how to patch things up after an argument, how to tell if an argument really can't be patched up, how to be part of a couple while remaining part of a wider group of friends, how to be part of a couple while remaining an individual, how to ask for attention without being possessive, how to survive rejection, and a lot more. For the most part, these lessons concerning the development of intimate relationships can be learned only firsthand, in the thick of things, by trying out or rehearsing various styles of interacting.

There's the other side of the coin, too: The teen who *doesn't* have a boyfriend/girlfriend might be suffering pangs of insecurity and unhappiness over the fact that everyone else in the world is pairing off. A boy worries he's retarded and out of it. A girl worries she'll never find love and no one will ever want to marry her. There's not a lot Mom or Dad can do about the situation, and asking questions—"Is there anybody you like right now?" or "How's the girlfriend scene these days?"—will likely just embarrass him, infuriate him, or add to his gloom. You may know that this bleak period will pass, life does go on, romantic partners will appear sooner or later; assuring a child of all that may help, but probably it won't. What *certainly* won't help much is saying something like, "You're so handsome and smart and nice, I don't understand why you don't have any dates."

Has my teen been kissed?

If you find out that your thirteen-year-old has been kissing his girlfriend and you don't approve, telling him to cut out this kissing business isn't going to stop him. So maybe you're better off not knowing. Don't ask.

But kissing, of course, is just the beginning and the most innocent aspect of burgeoning sexual interaction. No doubt you would reel off a few other questions that are on your mind and raising concerns:

- What do these kids do when they hang out at somebody's house after school?

- What do these kids do at the parties they have?

- Does my daughter let her boyfriend feel her up?

- Does my son try to get to third base with his girlfriend? Do kids talk about bases anymore?

You're not likely to hear much from your child by asking those questions. If your child wants to discuss his earliest physical experiences and get your opinions, knowledge, and perspective, that's a fine thing. Usually, however, teens do *not* want to. They don't want to talk about it because, one, they think sex is verboten in general; two, they believe Mom is going to run screaming from the room if she hears any specifics about the subject; three, sexual interactions put them in the adult world with Mom and Dad, and children of all ages really prefer not to think about their parents as sexual beings.

But here's a parent's appropriate role and effort in this loaded area of adolescent sexual behavior: You want to let your child know you'd be happy to talk things over with him if he wishes. You want to do what you can to help him learn to manage his social behaviors skillfully and with intelligent judgment. You want to be reassured that she can extricate herself from a tight spot without alienating everyone or putting herself in danger.

You can initiate conversations that enter those territories without zapping your child with pointed remarks or questions, such as, "I'm afraid you're screwing around." And it is right and good to initiate those conversations. Parents sometimes say, "I'm waiting for my child to bring this up or to come and ask me about all this." Well, guess what? You're going to keep on waiting. One of the useful effects of starting a conversation yourself can be to build up a little pressure on your child to share something that's uncomfortable for her, something she might actually wish to get out in the open. For example, often children who become drawn into oral sex activities or hooking up have feelings about those behaviors; they do know they're not completely okay. So you kind of read the silences, what she's not saying, and open the door for her to talk.

The mother of fourteen-year-old Jessica was "fairly horrified" thinking about the Saturday night parties her daughter was attending, "because sometimes I've picked her up after school and I see these kids hanging all over each other, so I can only imagine what goes on in these private homes." She wanted to ask her daughter, but one attempt at a conversation got nowhere: "How are the parties?" "Oh, they're fine." This is tough. You don't know what's going on, you're pretty sure it's not exactly what was going on back in your day, and you'd like to find out more without crossing the line into prying.

You're more likely to make a connection by beginning to talk about how your child *feels*, or what this kind of socializing is like for her, rather than pushing for details about her activities right off the bat. It's a perfect opportunity to tell a story or two on yourself.

Jessica's mom told her daughter about the little group of kids she hung out with in eighth grade, who all regularly held "birthday parties" at one girl's apartment because the girl's mother left them alone and they played kissing games like flashlight and spin the bottle with the lights out. At one such party, the generally acknowledged cutest boy in the group was challenged to kiss her with a mouthful of water: "He took a glass of water and filled up his mouth, then motioned me into the kitchen away from the other kids, spit out the water in the sink, and moved in on my lips. I didn't know what to do. So I turned my head and pointed to my cheek, he should kiss me on the cheek. Well, he was disgusted and I felt like a total jerk. Actually, all those parties were kind of stressful."

Jessica's mother continued: "Are the parties you've been going to enjoyable for you? I'm not trying to be nosy, I just remember what it was like for me and also I hear a lot on TV about stuff that happens today, and that scares me a little. Feel free to talk to me about any of that, I'm not going to be a judge and jury. If I can help in any way, I'd like to. Because I know sometimes I wished that my mom would have stepped in."

Jessica said: "Okay."

Mom said: "Come help me bake some cookies."

Relating her story, this mother said later, "It probably made me sound ancient to my daughter. I mean, I doubt these kids are into spin the bottle. But she did sort of chuckle." And Mom felt she'd promoted a welcoming atmosphere if Jessica did want to share some details of her own experiences later.

Many factors influence your child's decisions about sexual activities during these years—including his own sensitivities and beliefs, and what his peer group looks like. Think about how you can keep in touch and be available, without knowing all the details about the decisions he's reaching.

Is my child gay?

A teenager may have gay leanings or be attracted to members of the same sex, and I think parents don't necessarily need to know that, just as they don't need to know if a daughter has a boyfriend or a son has a girlfriend. A fair number of adolescents probably don't really know themselves whether or not they're gay.

I am not suggesting that a preference for a same-sex romantic or sexual partner is never real at this age. However, a number of factors—both cultural and developmental—make it possible that a teenager today isn't quite certain about the whole matter. Like much that's going on during adolescence, "gayness" may be transient, a matter of exploring, figuring out one's identity, and approaching the world in various ways. And since sexual orientation is discussed openly in some school classes, is the theme of popular TV shows, and in other ways has come onto children's radar screens from very early ages, young people are at least exposed to the model of possible relationships with same-sex partners. They know that same-sex relationships happen; often, they're able to acknowledge sexual feelings toward members of the same sex as well as toward the opposite sex.

For example, not a lot but a certain percentage of girls claim that they're attracted to other girls. The attraction, however, may not have a sexual context in the usual sense. When a girl tells me she's bisexual, I might ask, "Oh, really? Who are you sleeping with?" Answer: "Well, I don't sleep with anybody. I've never had sex." Patricia, eighteen, whom I'd seen off and on through her high school years, talked to me after returning from her first year away at college. There she discovered a phenomenon some kids referred to as lugs—lesbians until graduation. Two girls begin an intense involvement and conduct an affair that is not primarily sexual. Some sexual interactions may be involved, but that's not why the girls are in the relationship. Perhaps boys in college seem not to be as emotionally available as other girls are, and the "lesbian" relationship is a way of obtaining that form of intimacy.

One adolescent had been, in a sense, socialized into believing she was a lesbian. Sally, sixteen, came to therapy because, she said, she was depressed. I asked why, and she replied, "I'm depressed because I'm a lesbian, and I'm not sure I want to be one." Sally was a junior in high school, an all-state field hockey player, and a big girl with a sweet face. She had the body of a good field hockey player—large boned, well muscled, a kind of square shape. Our conversation went something like this:

Me: "What makes you say that you're a lesbian?"

Sally: "Some kids told me that I must be because of how I look."

Me: "Anything else?"

Sally: "Well, when I'm in the locker room with the other girls, I want to see what they look like, and I catch myself peeking at them in the shower."

Me: "Do you find that arousing? Any tingling sensations, or feelings you'd associate with being aroused?"

Sally: "Not particularly. I don't know that I'm aroused."

Me: "Do you fantasize or think about what boys look like with no clothes on?"

Sally: "Oh, all the time."

Me: "Do you see yourself going out on dates with boys or girls?"

Sally: "Boys."

Me: "If this was a boys' locker room, do you think you'd be peering around trying to get a glimpse of them?"

Sally: "Absolutely!"

I told Sally I didn't think she was a lesbian but was experiencing a normal curiosity about other people's bodies, including of the same sex. Sally was relieved.

A boy is less likely to acknowledge an attraction to other boys. One common perception holds that a teenage boy may know he's gay, but family and cultural attitudes prevent him from expressing his sexual preferences. To some extent, this prohibition does exist, and yet many gay males don't really come to that realization until the late teens or early twenties. In addition, we know that many males, perhaps as many as one in four or five, have a homosexual encounter at some point in their lives but are not gay despite that one experience.

An adolescent boy sometimes doesn't know what he wants or why he wants it. Perhaps he hopes to have sex with a girl because of how popular that will make him with his friends, or to erase the dreaded stigma of still being a virgin. In William S. Pollack's *Real Boys' Voices*, a sixteen-year-old explains, "Your virginity is the single most important thing that determines your social status in the eyes of almost every teenage male. In high school, virginity is a self-demeaning label that you want nothing more than to get rid of." A lot of boys, I believe, would be just as happy to stick with masturbation, than to confront the emotional intensity of being with a real girl.

My point in all this is that adolescents are sometimes confused themselves about the true nature of the attractions they experience toward others. But, of course, it's easy to appreciate a parent's curiosity or anxiety over a son's or daughter's sexual orientation. Any time a child decides to take a path that's out of the norm, or appears to be heading in that direction, parents typically have emotional reactions. In the case of a child's gayness, those reactions may run from "His life is going to be harder now" to "This means no grandchildren" to "What are the neighbors and the relatives going to say?" to "That's sick" to "That's a sin." Faced with such emotions, many parents prefer not to ask and not to know, and if the child does not bring up the issue himself, that may be a sensible attitude during these transition years. In fact, pressing for information about a child's sexual orientation or *suspected* sexual orientation may actually traumatize the child into not exploring what he's really feeling—in other words, into foreclosing that aspect of his identity in the direction that will please his parents.

When a teen *does* bring up the matter, or clearly wants to sound out his parents or gauge their reactions, it's almost always useful to encourage him to be open about his feelings and to try to maintain a calm response.

Has my teen been in trouble at school?

If you're aware that your adolescent has run into some trouble with a teacher, but he hasn't said much to you about it and the teacher hasn't considered it necessary to contact you, it's a safe assumption that both parties—teacher and student—are confident that the problem can be solved without parental intervention. So you don't need to know.

This is actually one of the stress-relieving, nerves-easing aspects of Stage 2 parenting, if you allow it to be: Your child's school life is increasingly largely out of your hands. Assuming he'll be moving out and on to college, it will soon be entirely out of your hands (aside from paying the bills), so that's one less thing for you to have to deal with. And very likely, he doesn't want to bring you in on much of anything that's going on in that part of his world.

Just as you don't necessarily need to hear about a reprimand, you don't need to know if your child has been singled out for praise or even an award at school. My daughter was something of a secret artist. One day during her junior high years, I bumped into another parent who said, "By the way, I really liked your daughter's painting in the art show. I'm glad it won first prize." My thought was, *What art show? What painting?* When I asked her about all this later, her response was, "Well, why would you guys be interested in that?"

Part of constructing one's identity as an adolescent is having secrets from Mom and Dad, even pleasant, self-aggrandizing secrets. It marks the transition from "Hey, Mom, and hey, Dad, look at the picture I drew, look what I did in school" to "I'm on my own, I have my own life, I don't have to tell you *everything* that's going on, do I?"

Has my child been rejected by a formerly friendly clique at school?

Looking back, said Amy, a sixteen-year-old junior in high school, seventh grade "was absolutely the pits, the worst year ever. This little group of girls just started totally ignoring me, and two of them had actually been my friends." Amy remembered spending a lot of time in her bedroom, alone, watching "stupid cartoons on TV." Her mother asked her often what was wrong. Amy said, "I really didn't want to talk to her about all that stuff, because there wasn't anything she could do about it. Plus, she'd probably give me some lame advice." Finally, Amy did tell her mom a few details and got lame advice. "She said, well why don't you just say this or just say that, and you should forget about those girls anyway, they're just mean kids. I know she wanted to help, but really it didn't help."

Many children, after the fact, speak about seventh grade as a bad year, a time of unpleasant teasing, mean gossiping, and ostracizing. If your child seems to be on the receiving end of that behavior and is suffering, certainly as a loving parent you want to show that you care, indicate that you're available if she wants to talk, and maybe indulge you both in a shopping trip or a dinner out. But the truth is, teens have to struggle through their passing social upheavals largely on their own. They often don't want to talk about the whole miserable business. And parents often don't remember how miserable it truly is; "forget about those girls, get together with some other kids" sounds reasonable.

But adolescents have two overriding fears: the fear of humiliation and the fear of invisibility, both related to developing identity. The quest for identity is really the desire to have *being*, to know you exist and to know that other people know you exist. When a child says to her peers, in effect, "Here's who I am," and they reply, in effect, "Yuck!" or "Who? What? We don't see anybody," her identity is challenged. Being ignored is one of the worst things that can happen, not only because it feels lonely but also because it negates a child's being.

This is why children in these transition years so greatly fear abandonment and exclusion, and suffer from it to a degree adults probably can't appreciate. In my therapy group, if a child doesn't show up for a session, I might call her in a couple of days and ask, "Where were you last week? We missed you." Invariably, she's astounded and thrilled that someone actually noticed she wasn't there. It's a poignant emotion. As a parent of a rejected teen, sometimes your most helpful stance is to convey the message, "I'm here and I know you're there, and let's do something nice together."

Is my daughter secretly putting on makeup after she leaves the house for school?

Or rolling up the waistband of her little school uniform to turn it into a micro-miniskirt?

Here's a classic instance of why it's so important to pick the mountain you'll die on. Think ahead. You don't want to destroy your relationship with your daughter over lip gloss or eight inches of exposed thigh. Make a big deal over such matters, and there's nothing left for when the really big deals come and you need that relationship to be sturdy and intact. You have no traction, because you've burned it up over a relatively unimportant issue. So maybe it's better not to know what she does to her appearance once she leaves the house.

Of course, you and your child may not agree on what's important. Your daughter may think that going out in a scoop-neck T-shirt not wearing a bra is fine. You may think, indeed know, that the consequences of going braless are wider than she may understand. If you do feel strongly that it's appropriate for you to have some say in how she dresses, you need to explain your concern. Reason is the track to take. She still may not agree, but at least you don't come off sounding completely arbitrary. If you say, "I don't want you going out wearing that," her response will likely be, "Why not? Everybody dresses like this." Probably she's right. What happens, of course, is that girls become competitive, and there can be a kind of race to see who can wear the least clothes, who dares to be the most revealing. It's also true, as one mother said, "Kids and parents have a different vocabulary. To me, some of the clothes my daughter likes are trashy or what used to be called slutty. To her, they're cool."

Convey a message that says, "I don't really want to tell you what to do, but I do want you to know a few things and understand a concern that I have." Start with the positive. Mom might say, "You're a very attractive young woman. Of course, in my mind you're still my baby, but I'm sure that a lot of boys think you're hot and sexy. I know it's gratifying to feel that way, and to get attention, but you have to be a little careful. You may get stared at or talked to by men you pass on the street. Boys may try to touch your body, and you don't want them to. So this is why I get worried about some of the ways you dress. What do you think about that?"

You still may hear the protests ("All my friends wear stuff like this"). Then it's appropriate to say, "I understand that, but I've explained why I'm concerned. We'll have to compromise. The shirt's all right but you must wear a bra."

Is my son looking at pictures of nude adults in magazines or on the Internet?

Stumble across some *Playboy* magazines in your teen's room, and probably you're upset. You're upset because the realization that he's looking at nude pictures means, one, your little boy is growing up, which means you're getting old; and two, now, you think, you're going to have to deal with the *Playboy* issue, which means the sex issue, in one way or another. Before, you didn't know; now it's out there, and you feel it's incumbent on you to address it.

When I talk to parents who are concerned about nude pictures, I usually start off with one of my favorite questions: "What were you doing at that age?" Half say, "Oh, God, yeah, I was doing that, but that doesn't make it right." I reply, "Well, let's consider. Did looking at nude pictures turn you into an evil person? Destroy your life?"

No, it didn't.

So the first thing is, don't panic. The second thing is, is it really incumbent on you to say something to your child or to attempt to find out if he's sneaking even more *Playboys* into the house?

Throughout this book I come back to the point that concerning many of your child's secret behaviors—the ones you think you need to say something about—you can buy a little time. If an adolescent is downloading bomb-making equipment or Mom discovers a Glock knife under the pillow, that's trouble. Those are actively and virulently dangerous behaviors. One more *Playboy* magazine, one more nude picture, however, is not going to turn your child into a sex maniac. It's all part of figuring out sexual identity, experiencing sexual arousal, and seeing what the other half of the world looks like without clothes on. So it's probably best to bite your tongue and say nothing.

A somewhat related side note: Starting in early adolescence, girls become desperate to start shaving their legs, a major rite of passage. And parents often are resistant, for reasons they can't quite explain themselves. What they're feeling is ambivalence. As with the boy who wants to look at nude pictures, the girl who wants to shave her legs is Mom and Dad's little girl advancing to adulthood.

Does my child masturbate?

The short answer is: probably.

Here are some thoughts and/or worries that may be going through your child's mind:

- Does everybody do this?

- Masturbate sounds like a dirty word. Why do they call it that?

- Is it wrong or creepy that it feels so good?

- Is doing this once a week normal?

- Maybe I'm not doing it right.

- How do I know what's right, because the one time I asked my friend he started laughing and calling me a perv?

- My best friend says she masturbates all the time and it's terrific, and our biology book says people do it all the time, but I've never done it and I don't want to, so does that mean there's something wrong with me?

These are private thoughts or worries. If your child requests your answer to them, that's fine. If she doesn't, it's probably better not to question her about the matter. For one thing, it's easy for a parent to make a child feel guilty about masturbating, even without intending to do so. If accidentally discovering a child in the act, for example, it's an understandable parental instinct to react as if we're furious about the whole business. Merry, fourteen, described this incident, from a time she was about ten:

"The steps in back of our house have iron railings along the sides, and this one day I was just hanging around back there and trying to see if I could slide down a railing, like you see somebody sliding down a bannister in the movies. Well, I didn't slide, but when I was kind of straddling the railing I started to get these exciting feelings so I kept sort of pulling myself up and down, rubbing myself against the railing. Just then my mom walked out and saw me and looked totally shocked. She said, 'What are you doing?' in this loud, scary, sort of angry voice. So I knew what I was doing was a bad, bad thing."

Maybe Merry's mother believed masturbation was a bad, bad thing. Maybe that wasn't it at all, and she simply was startled, a little nonplussed, and blurted out her question without thinking. But a negative message was conveyed, and children pick up negative messages from adults and other grown-ups in their lives in various ways. A little boy enjoys walking around pulling on his penis, and Dad or Grandma takes his hand away, offers him a toy or a snack as distraction, or tells him that penis pulling should be carried on only in his own room. So kids, boys and girls, can grow up feeling furtive about using their bodies in these ways.

When a child is young, it's actually a good idea to convey the message, "You might like to touch or rub your genitals, and that might feel good, and that's a normal thing to do in private." When he reaches the highly self-conscious, self-absorbed, easily embarrassed preteen and teen years, any such comment from his parents will be excruciatingly mortifying.

Has my child ever had a beer? Smoked cigarettes?

To expect your child to traverse adolescence without being exposed to alcohol and tobacco and giving them a try is, I think, folly. You don't have to condone drinking and smoking, but neither do you need to know every time he's had a bottle of Amstel or puffed a Marlboro.

However, since drinking and smoking negatively affect safety and health, it's perfectly appropriate and good-parent-like to talk about the issues with your child and also to gather information about what goes on in his crowd or what he's exposed to. This is one of those subjects about which you can do a little reconnaissance, just sort of flying over the area. I'm fond of the let-me-tell-you-a-story-about-me approach. For example, you might say, "When I went to school, there was lots of drinking. This was before pot, but practically every kid had some beer." Relate a beer-drinking incident in your past. Then ask, "What's it like in your school? Do a lot of kids seem to drink? Is it something the school talks about?" Listen to what he has to say.

If your child is heading off to a party: "Are the kids allowed to have beer?" Maybe the reply is, "Oh, Mom, don't be silly." Or maybe, "Well, there'll probably be some beer, but that's not really my thing." Then it's a good idea to forge on anyway, and say, "I'm glad to hear that. Is there some way we can help you to keep staying away from drinking at these parties? It is better not to. And you do know, of course, that it's illegal to drink, even beer, at your age."

Regarding cigarettes, take an adult-to-adult approach to your conversation. You might say, "You've heard all the facts about smoking a thousand times, I don't have to tell you that it's bad for you. So I just want you to know I don't want you to smoke. I understand that socially you might feel compelled to have cigarettes, if other kids are doing it, but remember that smoking just isn't a smart thing to do."

What You Do Need to Know

It's not difficult to see that certain of these Mom-and-Dad-don't-need-to-know behaviors fall toward the benign end of a continuum—which has an infinitely more worrisome opposite end.

If you don't need to know that your teenager is in a black funk because a boyfriend broke up with her, you do need to know if she's seriously depressed for some reason.

You don't need to know if your son has been reprimanded by a teacher, but you do need to know if he's in chronic trouble at school or hasn't been showing up there at all.

A few *Playboy* magazines stuffed behind his desk aren't cause for great concern. Looking at extremely pornographic film clips or communicating with strangers on the Internet may be.

Drinking a beer isn't too worrisome. Abusing drugs or alcohol is extremely worrisome.

You don't need to get all the facts about boy girl parties. You do need to know if your son or daughter is being physically or sexually abused or is abusing others.

It's probably safe to assume that being dropped by a former friend is a painful experience your child can struggle through on her own, but if persistent mean teasing or bullying is going on, she may need your help.

So how do you determine when secretive behaviors should start legitimately worrying you and prompt you to take action, at least by attempting to uncover more information?

Many parenting advice materials offer "the checklist," red flags for parents to watch out for—from a change in sleeping and eating patterns to loss of interest in formerly enjoyed activities to dropping old friends. The warning-signs model, however, tends both to oversimplify things and to incline a parent to jump in with both feet before getting a truly clear picture. That's when Mom or Dad pops up one evening in the child's bedroom and says, "You're showing four of the eight red flags. I know you're in trouble and we have to do something right now!" And the teenager thinks, *What are you talking about? You just read some list and you decided I'm a nutcase? Don't you trust me or know me?*

Of course, sometimes parents are right. The red flags are there; they shouldn't be ignored. The trick is to inform yourself further while also trying to open up communication with your child. You might find it useful to ask yourself:

"How long has the worrisome behavior been going on?" Duration is important. Part of the construction of identity is that adolescents try on various personae and go through various emotional stages. So anything out of the ordinary that's lasting more than a month or two is probably worth noting.

Where and when is he acting in this way I don't much like? If he's moody and dreary around the house but comes to life when his friends enter the scene, maybe he's not as seriously depressed as you fear.

How does he react when I express a little concern? How angry is your child at your attempts to learn more about what he's up to? Saying, "Mom, just leave me alone, okay?" is fairly normal. Saying, "If you come in my room I'll kill you," is a clue that you're on to something important.

How dramatic is the reversal in my child's behavior? It's one thing for a parent to say, "My child has always loved classical music, but now it's gangsta rap he listens to and I'm really worried that he's going to hell in a handbasket." That conclusion we might safely say is an overreaction. It's quite another to observe, "My child used to love music, but now he just sits and stares out the window, sleeps a lot, and doesn't seem interested in much of anything."

Can I get some corroboration of what I think is going on? Has your child's teacher, other parents, other relatives been noticing the same signals you've picked up?

And always, start with your child. See what he'll tell you. Remember that conversations don't have to go on at length the minute he walks in the door looking vaguely unhappy. You say: "How was the party?" Child: mumble, mumble. You: "Well, that doesn't sound like much fun." Child: mumble, mumble. You: "Okay, good night, dear." Maybe the next day you come back and say, "You know, last night when we talked, it sounded like you didn't have a really good time with your friends."

In Chapter 6, "Real Trouble," I return to what you do need to know and take a closer look at the other end of the continuum—how to handle it when an adolescent's secretive behaviors have crossed into dangerous territory and the child needs help. But first, in the next chapter, about "Rules, Boundaries, and When and How to Confront Your Teen," I explore some more ideas on how to keep checking in without prying.

At the end of the day, you are the parent and you have the right to ask questions, to set limits, and to impose consequences. In some cases, you must. In many parent-teen relationships, however, Mom or Dad's comments and expressions of concern seem to the child to come completely out of the blue, although Mom or Dad may actually have been agonizing over the issue at hand for weeks or months. Some of the strategies I look at next can help you avoid the out-of-the-blue moment that your adolescent is bound to resent.

CHAPTER 5

Lines in the Sand

*Rules, Boundaries, and When and
How to Confront Your Teen*

While you and your preteen or teen are in the process of renegotiating your shared lives over these years, there will come a time—many times—when you'll want to establish basic ground rules. As a parent, it's proper for you to set boundaries on your child's behavior and activities, including some of those aspects of his personal life that he would prefer to keep secret and within his exclusive control. But if you try to impose rules in a unilateral manner, you come across as an irrational power wielder and are in danger of effectively losing your child's trust and even admiration.

This is why I encourage parents to come up with rules jointly with their adolescents. Again, as I suggested earlier, all such kinds of talk ideally will take place well in advance of the time your fifteen-year-old arrives home late for the second night in a row, you have no idea where she's been, and you slap her with two weeks' grounding. Set up a pattern for interacting over issues relating to her privacy and her insistence on her right to run her own life before you really need to.

Say something like, "Soon you'll be starting to go off more on your own and spend more time with your friends, and we will have to make some guidelines about all that. I'll tell you what I think those should be, and I want to hear your opinions—what you believe would be a reasonable rule to set and what would be a reasonable consequence if the rule gets broken." The notion is, "Here's what *I'm* putting out on the table, what do *you* want to bring to the table? Here's the agreement I think we probably should have about curfews/attending parties/use of the computer/beer drinking/me going into your room when you're not there. What do you think?"

In such a conversation, at a time when there's no major trouble afoot, you have a sterling opportunity to explain your reasons for what might seem to your child like poking around in his private life. You can mention certain actions you undoubtedly will take at some unknown point in the future. So you might say, "Look, I do want to be kept informed about where you're going, and sometimes I'll ask you to tell me. This is for my information and reassurance, and not because I'm prying and being nosy."

Or: "I will need to see your report card and generally keep tabs on how you're doing in school. Just because you're in eighth grade now, you can't say your school grades are private."

Or: "I'm going to be warning you about driving with some of your friends under certain circumstances. It's not you I'm worried about, it's the others." (Which is true sometimes, although not always.)

In the heat of a moment—or when trouble *is* afoot—it's almost inevitable for an adolescent to think, *Yeah, sure, Mom says it's not about trust, but really she doesn't trust me to walk around the block by myself.* When you tell your child in advance what you expect from him, what you might do, and why you'll be doing it, you take away the weight of that protest. He remembers, maybe reluctantly, that you did explain all this earlier.

In corporations and other aspects of adult life, the most effective leader is generally the individual who solicits opinions, who says, "What do you think?" to the others in the group. And then, "On the basis of everything you've said, here's what I've decided to do." This is an excellent parental leadership strategy. As you engage in a little back-and-forth negotiation, sometimes you'll hear input from your child that you can accept; sometimes not. Teens don't always have a plan or well-thought-out suggestions about rules, but you should always ask for them. Maybe your child does have an idea, and it sounds to you like not a particularly good one. In that case, you might feel comfortable saying, "Well, I'm not convinced that's a great idea, but let's start with that and see how it goes."

Often, you can include a component of what your teen comes up with: "Okay, you think midnight is a good time for you to be home. We can't do that as a general rule, but depending on where you are and what's going on right then, we might be able to say okay this one time." Adolescents can be pretty receptive to the fine art of give-and-take; they can appreciate your willingness to go along with one request but not another: "You may have a party and you and your friends can be downstairs by yourselves, but you're not allowed to have the lights off."

Try to create some goodwill while you can—which isn't giving in. Goodwill means demonstrating that you'll listen to opposing arguments and you're open to discussion about these issues, though you will be the final arbiter.

Behind all of this, essentially, is an effort to nurture and foster your child's thoughts about appropriate behavior and to teach him how to draw his own boundaries—because the teens who get in the most difficulty are the ones who haven't learned to do so. The process starts right there, at home, in the talks you and your child have about ground rules and from the suggestions you make. They remain only suggestions; you cannot compel your adolescent to act in ways you want him to. But with thoughtful negotiating on your part, the twain can meet somewhere in the middle when your teen wants to hear a yes and you'd feel happier giving him a no.

In this chapter, I talk also about some thornier issues, when you think you have reason to worry in earnest. Your child may be telling you nothing about his secret life, but you suspect something is going on that you should know about. Maybe you've stumbled across "evidence" of possible trouble. Maybe you know your child has lied to you about a particular incident. How do you confront your teen with your concerns? Should you? All the examples I look at in this chapter fall within the range of normal adolescent behavior—which doesn't mean they're not going to cause parents grief.

Most adolescents really don't want to be a huge disappointment to their parents. They just stop knowing how to please them, because mothers and fathers so often sound simply scared and/or accusatory ("Where are you going? What are you doing? Can I trust you?"). Some ideas on how to improve that picture follow, starting with setting up ground rules and moving on to the weightier matters of secret stashes and bold-faced lies.

Setting Curfews

Some parents stand by a regular curfew, the hour at which their child is expected to be home. Some impose or adjust a curfew as a consequence for a previous trashing of the rules. In either case, according to an adolescent's way of thinking, his parents issue curfews in order to prevent him from enjoying life. He is unaware of the concerns, worries, or abject terrors about what might happen to him "out there" that are flitting through his parent's mind and that will be eased only when he walks intact through the door once again. At eleven P.M.

It's sometimes assumed that when a therapist works with a teenager and her family, he's focusing on attempting to get the parents to understand their child. However, I often aim to have the teen try to understand her parents, because if she can do that, her behaviors may become more reasonable, less random, and based on particular goals. When I meet with teenagers, I sometimes say to these adolescents who are now in some ways adults, "Look, you're not doing a very good job of managing your parents. You don't get what's actually going on with them, and they just seem like irrational psychotics. Let me try to explain what's almost surely passing through their tiny little minds."

To give a demonstration, I might use the following imagined, very typical, conversation between Jennie and her mom, after Jennie has just come in from seeing a movie with her friends:

Mom: "Jennie, you know you had to be home by eleven and here it is twelve."

Jennie: "You just made that rule because you know all the movies let out at eleven-fifteen so there's no way I could be home by eleven. Nobody has a curfew of eleven, so I can never go to a movie, because you don't want me to have any friends!"

Now, if I asked Jennie's mother why she was concerned when her daughter wasn't home on time, she might explain, "Well, I'd immediately think she's been in an accident or she's been kidnapped, and it's probably all her father's and my fault because we've been horrible parents."

Jennie's response to this explanation would probably be, "What? What on earth are you talking about?" Jennie had no idea. It still sounds ridiculous to her, but at least now she has some inkling of why her mother made such a big deal about twelve o'clock versus eleven o'clock.

Your adolescent is self-absorbed enough, in a completely healthy way, *not* to be wondering what you're thinking. But you can tell her; in fact, expressing the real concerns on your mind is a key transition into Stage 2 parenting. Once she hears what those concerns are, it's harder for her to assume that you're just out to ruin her life and not let her have any privacy at all. You want your child not only to respect the rules but also to appreciate how and why the rules are set. She may not agree with them, but she sees that you're trying to respect her opinion and her wishes.

Here's a key concept to keep in mind when setting curfews or laying down any other rules that your child feels will put a crimp in her private life: People in general, and adolescents in particular, confuse agreement and understanding. Your teen believes that if you truly *understand* what she's saying, you will naturally *agree* with her. Therefore, because you're not agreeing, it must mean you don't understand. The dialogue sounds like this:

Mom: "You're supposed to be home by eleven. That's the legal curfew and that's the rule we set."

Daughter: "But Mom, you don't get it. I just explained to you, the movies don't let out until eleven-fifteen. Get it now?" This is somewhat like the instinct to talk slower and louder to a person who speaks a foreign language.

If mom keeps insisting on eleven, daughter thinks, *My parents are so stupid, they don't understand anything.* The reality is, Mom does *understand*, she just doesn't *agree*. So parents need to be crystal clear and say in so many words: "I heard you, I understand what you're saying, I can repeat it back to you if you want, and I appreciate why you feel that way. However, I can't agree. We're not going to agree on everything, and this is

one of those times. I heard what you said, and I know it's difficult for you to stick by this rule, but that's not why I'm making
the rule. I'm making the rule because I'm responsible for you."

Help your child understand you better. It can make the
business of jointly coming up with acceptable curfews go a little more smoothly.

Then, you might mull over in your mind a few questions:

**Does it make sense to have one curfew for all occa-
sions?** If eleven o'clock is the time you want to see your child
back home every night, can you live with some exceptions to
the rule? If all the movies *do* let out at eleven-fifteen, do you
need to take that into consideration?

**Can I rely on my child to decide a reasonable hour to
be home?** A wonderful dialogue between parent and adolescent sounds like this: Mom says, "Okay, so you're going to the
basketball game at school this evening and then you want to
hang out with your friends at the coffee shop. What do you
think is a fair time for me to expect you home?" Child says,
"Well, the game will probably be over around ten. How about
eleven-fifteen?" Mom says, "Fine, we'll agree on that." This
parent, knowing what she does about her daughter based on
recent history, trusts her to be reasonable and stick by their
agreement.

But some teens angrily resist being pinned down and consider a parent's insistence a gross invasion of their freedom and
privacy and an insult to their burgeoning adulthood. Christine, fifteen, was furious at her mother; the two had had a
major battle over Christine's wish to go to a Saturday night
party at a friend's house—and no curfews. Here's how Christine described her feelings: "She's always at me about how I
have to be more responsible. So for this whole week before the
party I did everything I was supposed to do. Like, I fed the cat
every morning and night and changed the litter box. I brought

all my soda cans and stuff into the kitchen. I put all my clothes in the laundry and the towels back in the bathroom. I showed her I was totally responsible. So she should trust me enough to be responsible about getting home from this party."

In Christine's mind, five days of admirable pet care and bedroom cleanup proved she could be allowed to make her own curfew decisions. I would guess that Christine's mother had good cause to believe that this sudden display of responsibleness wasn't something she could bank on in the larger realm of her daughter's life. You have to know your child and how much she realistically requires in terms of your guidance and boundaries. A nice response from Christine's mother might have been, "I've noticed how you've been getting all your chores done this week. Good for you! Applause, applause! I appreciate it. So does the cat. And now let's see what decision we need to make about your going to this party and when you'll be home."

Can I arrange a check-in time with my generally trustworthy child? Here's where a parent might say, "If you're going to be late, you need to tell me because I start worrying. Let's agree to set a curfew at eleven, and if you're going to be more than fifteen minutes late, you'll call and let me know where you are. And it's always okay. Remember that I can always come get you if necessary. If you want, we can have a code word—you'll tell me over your cell phone that you're really tired or something. So you won't have to say in front of your friends, 'Mom, come get me.' How does that sound?"

If my child does get home at the required hour, do I need to know where she was? When your child reaches the years of middle adolescence, maybe you don't need to know. And maybe not asking is an excellent way of both preserving her wish for privacy and ensuring that the curfew rule is adhered to. My daughter learned early on that if she got home on time, we wouldn't ask her where she'd been. So she always came in on time. This was an agreement that evolved, not one we ever talked out in so many words.

Double-Checking

Thirteen-year-old Emma told her mother one Friday morning that she was planning to go to her friend Betsy's house after school, and the two would spend the weekend there working on a class project. Betsy's parents would be home; Emma and Betsy were going to rent videos to watch in the evenings and they might do a little shopping Saturday afternoon. All this was fine with Emma's mom, who then said to her daughter, "Okay, I'm just going to call Betsy's mother to make sure she'll be there over the weekend." Emma responded with fury, "You don't believe me, do you? What, you think we're secretly planning to invite in a bunch of guys and have a wild party? That's the trouble, you never believe me!"

I have heard variations of this exchange from countless teens. But as the parent of a young adolescent, it's part of your role to know where your child is, whom she's with, and usually, in a situation such as the one Emma was going into, if parents or other responsible adults will be on the premises. It was appropriate for Emma's mother to want to be sure that two thirteen-year-old girls wouldn't be alone in an empty house for three days. One way this kind of parental fact-finding can be made more palatable to a child is to present it as a matter of double checking.

Emma's mother might answer her daughter's outburst this way: "Yes, I do believe you. But my job is to double-check. It's not a question of my not trusting you, this is just how I'm going to operate, because I do it for myself. I need to reassure myself that you'll be okay."

Talking about "double-checking, although I know you're telling me the truth" sounds very different to an adolescent than Mom or Dad "checking up" on her.

As with all rules and boundaries, it's good to lay this one out before a situation arises: "Sometimes when you're staying with a friend, I'm going to want to double-check with her parents to be sure everybody knows what the plans are." What I often hear from parents, however, is that Mom or Dad and the teen got into a standoff—child shouting, "You never trust me!" parent insisting, "I do trust you!" and nobody feeling happy. The parent wanted to say the right thing, but ended up feeling that the situation wasn't handled well. It can be useful to revisit that unsatisfactory scene sometime later, when everyone has cooled down. I know that parents absolutely loathe having to do so; who wants to risk starting another big argument?

But try this: "Remember on Saturday night, we got into a battle about me calling Katie's mom and you thought I was checking up on you? Let's go over that again, because I think it's really important. I was concerned not because I didn't trust you or I thought you weren't being honest with me. I wasn't checking up on you, I was double-checking. I needed to call to make myself feel more comfortable about the arrangements."

Adolescents don't especially *like* that explanation, but they do hear it.

Double checking might mean getting more information about your child's school performance. She's been telling you everything's just super, but you're pretty sure you're not getting the whole picture and you're concerned. Probably it's unwise to go rummaging through her backpack when she's out at the store, searching for evidence of academic failure or other school difficulties. But you want to know if others' stories match up with your child's, either to put your mind at ease or to uncover a problem you might be missing. There's nothing wrong with telling your teen you need to double-check to be sure you're doing all you can to be of help if she needs help, and so you'll be giving her teacher or counselor a call to get feedback about her schoolwork.

The Hovering Parental Presence

Often it's an excellent idea to let your child understand you're nearby—not *too* nearby and not visible, but somewhere on the perimeter of the scene. You may know that your child is honest and trustworthy, but perhaps he's at a stage or of a nature that suggests he may get in difficulty in a particular situation. Preempt that if you can.

In my son's high school, "beach week" was an established celebration of graduation. Several seniors would rent a cottage or apartment at the beach and luxuriate in their freedom for five days. Parents, of course, universally regarded this practice with alarm. When it came my son's time for beach week, I said, "Guess what? Good news! Your mom and I are able to take some time off and have a little holiday of our own. So we're going to the beach too that week. We're not going to stay with you, we've rented a place some distance away, and here's the rule: Once a day, we'll stop by. Just to look in, make sure you don't need anything. This will be at a time of your choosing, and you can call us in the morning and tell us when that would be."

The teens were on their own, but a parental presence was nearby. There would be no sneak attacks from us in the form of surprise drop-ins. Once a day, they had to make the place presentable; if they wanted to hide incriminating evidence of one sort or another, they could. And these adolescents were really wonderful about the plan. They did not object; we stopped by briefly as promised. At the same time, we were honoring them as being accountable and respecting their privacy.

Cell phones can help in creating a hovering parental presence. If you're anticipating that your child will be in a tricky situation, say you'd like her to check in with you on a regular basis. Or call her, thoroughly embarrassing her, just to say hi (then listen to what's going on in the background). The aim is not necessarily to catch her out but to remind her that you're there and to keep yourself informed.

One of the good effects of letting your child know you're on the perimeter of the scene is that she might actually be reassured by your presence—though she'll never tell you so. Children at this age still have some throwback feelings to the little kids they used to be, like wanting to know that Mom's in the house. You're offering your child an invisible safety net, which isn't *entirely* invisible to her.

To Snoop or Not to Snoop

Give your child a chance to prove himself to you. Assume innocence. This is one of the beauties of democracy, after all, and we should give our children the same benefit of the doubt that our government is instructed to offer us.

One powerful way is to allow him the privacy of his own room, which of course he is insisting on anyway. If he abuses being allowed to maintain this sanctuary without much outside interference, you'll have to do something about it (more on this later). But don't anticipate that he's going to abuse it.

I listened to the following exchange between sixteen-year-old Frank and his mother, who had been having volatile disagreements about Frank's comings and goings. The issue up for discussion was Frank's bedroom.

Frank: "Okay, let's be explicit. What are the rules about my room? When will you come in?"

Mom: "I'll come in whenever I please. You're still a child, Frank, you live under our roof, we pay all your bills, and until that changes, I have the right to go in your room whenever I want."

That was not a good answer, although certainly this parent was correct about who owned the house and who paid the bills. When, where, or why a child's room or personal possessions should be off-limits to his parents is one of the matters that can be negotiated or explained. Frank's mom might have said something like, "Here's why I would come into your room. I come in to put your laundry away. I come in once a week to run a vacuum through the two-foot-square space in the center of your floor that's relatively free of debris. I come in when I'd like to talk to you. I'm more than happy to knock first. I won't go through your drawers or desk or closet. But I want you to know there are some things I worry about, like whether you might be hiding alcohol in your room. Things like that, which I think all parents worry about. If I have any reason to believe that might be happening, I will need to violate this rule about staying out of your room unless you invite me in or unless I'm just doing basic household chores. So that's the deal. What do you think about it?"

You're letting your child know that you consider it part of your job to protect him, and possibly the time will come when that involves looking around his room or calling other parents to get information or finding out what he's up to on the computer. But you're sure that won't be necessary because you have confidence and trust in his good judgment. Get across the idea that by keeping some reasonable tabs on him, you'll be allaying your own anxieties and avoiding more furtive prying and snooping about his business.

Working Behind the Scenes, Setting Boundaries

You can shape your child's environment somewhat in ways that will influence her behavior along a safe course of action, without alienating her or invading her space or suggesting you don't trust her.

Limit and monitor her cash flow. Some teenagers are given so much pocket money that it's entirely too easy and tempting to buy drugs. It's a good idea to talk over with your child how much money she reasonably needs—for food, movies, CDs, and clothing—and stick to that. Keep an eye on where and how quickly she spends.

Limit her choices. Most teens will experiment with danger if it presents itself but won't particularly go out looking for it. Limiting the kinds of temptation to which your child may be vulnerable is a painless way to keep her safer. Keep alcohol, if you have it, out of reach of children, perhaps in a locked cabinet. Lock up guns, if you possess them, or remove them from your home. Use the parental control options offered by your Internet access provider.

Don't leave the house every weekend and expect your child to stay home alone. Fifteen-year-old Devon talked about feeling pressured to have sex with her boyfriend. Devon's mother was divorced and was herself dating at the time, and Devon was often on her own in the evenings. She would "die," Devon said, before she discussed her sex problems with her mom. Then she added, quite poignantly, "You know, things would be a lot easier for me if I didn't have all this freedom." Sometimes, simply having less opportunity to be sexually active means that sex doesn't happen—to the teenager's relief. Devon was saying she'd feel more comfortable if her mom was around more, maybe being a hovering parental presence when Devon's boyfriend wanted to come over.

When You Find Something You Didn't Want to Find

What might you turn up in your child's room that would push your panic buttons? That might be a six-pack of Amstel in the back of his closet, drug paraphernalia, condoms. Take it as a sign of something going on—but not necessarily a catastrophe in the making.

The first step is to handle your emotions so that they do not prevent you from thinking ahead. Thinking ahead means asking yourself: "What do I fear and what do I want to accomplish?" Be very careful about when you decide to blow your cover, because once you reveal that you've found what your child has hidden in his room, you lose your ability to find anything in the future. Your child immediately becomes more secretive. The six-pack or the condoms may still be in his life, just not anywhere for you to find.

Generally it's unwise to be uncovering items in an adolescent's room, but sometimes you can't help but see them. In fact, there is truth to the notion that occasionally children at some level do want to be found out. And if they do, they will continue leaving stuff for Mom or Dad to trip over.

Luke's mother found a marijuana joint in her son's jeans when she emptied the pockets in order to throw the pants in the wash. Not knowing quite what to do about it, she tossed out the joint and said nothing. The following week a joint showed up again in the pocket of the jeans.

So she questioned Luke, and his reply was, "Oh, I was just holding that for a friend." (This is the universal answer to be expected from a teen in such a situation.) His mom said, "Well, all right, but you shouldn't leave this kind of thing in your pocket, because it's dangerous, you might get caught with it. Frankly, also, I've got to tell you that it makes me wonder if *you're* smoking pot. You know, a lot of kids would say they're just keeping something for a friend."

Luke: "Okay, okay."

The next week, another joint appeared in the jeans pocket. At that point she realized her son did have a problem and she needed to take matters to another level. But if this parent had exploded in fear and anger on first finding the marijuana ("What's this?! Don't ever smoke this stuff!"), she might not have had that opportunity later on. The chances are good that Luke, sensing that his parent was no more able to handle this matter of his pot smoking than he was, would have made sure his mom never caught him again. And no discussion would have taken place.

This mother was able to say, "Luke, I think you're sending me a message, because we talked about this before and you keep leaving a joint in your pocket for me to find. I'm concerned. Let's sit down, your dad and you and me, and talk about it and figure out the best way to handle this." The three of them did, and it was decided they would all meet with a counselor and get some advice. It's often useful, by the way, to have the other parent or perhaps another concerned adult present during any confrontation, to maintain calm and encourage productive communication.

One helpful thought to remember: Adolescence is a time when self-destructive behaviors may be tried and toyed with. In fact, studies have shown that *most* teenage boys—and this is by self-reports or their own admissions—dabble in illegal activities (which of course includes having a few beers when they're sixteen). It's pretty normal behavior. What matters is what stays and what fades away as your child matures, and what part you play in that evolution.

When You Might Want to Go Undercover for a While

One of my repeated mantras throughout this book: Sometimes you need to bide your time. When faced with what looks like a troubling secret on your child's part, it can be useful not to show your hand too early. Gather information before you take action.

This is a sensible approach if you stumble across a joint or a beer can, but not if you discover something you consider to be extremely serious. Lying low isn't *always* the right idea. If you find a gun stashed in the back of your son's closet, obviously you won't wait around for further information.

What's serious and not so serious is partly up to the parent's judgment. If you know your child is by nature reckless or makes poor decisions as a rule, you don't want to let evidence of a risk-taking behavior go by for long. If a child has asthmatic attacks and has been advised by his doctor that smoking will be significantly more dangerous than for the average teen, finding a joint or cigarettes in that boy's pocket is pretty serious. For one parent, discovering a diaphragm in her daughter's drawer might be extremely worrisome; another parent might experience relief (*at least she's not going to get pregnant*). Going undercover or not also has something to do with the kind of relationship you have established with your child over the years. One mother who finds K-Y Jelly and a diaphragm in her daughter's room might be comfortable saying right off, "Hey, I saw this in your drawer. What's up?"

However, in many situations and for the majority of parents, it works better to go undercover briefly and see what else can be learned. The mother who finds the diaphragm might think, *All right, I have a little bit of intelligence here. Maybe it's a good idea to start from there and gather a few more facts or impres-*

sions. She might just observe her daughter more closely for a while, see whom she's hanging out with or on the phone with a lot. Mom gives some thought to how certain she is that her child is where she says she is in the afternoons after school. Maybe she calls the teacher who monitors the extracurricular debate team that meets once a week and asks how Molly has been doing, and the teacher mentions that Molly missed the last couple of sessions.

All this is building a case—so that when you *do* confront your child, first, you're able to express your concern (fairly calmly) around specific information you're responding to, and second, it's not so easy for your child to get away with the stock response that it's someone else's diaphragm.

When confronted, when her back is up against the wall, a teen's instinct—in addition to denial of any culpability—is to suggest that you don't know what you're talking about.

In my groups for adolescents, one of my rules is that no one can arrive drunk or stoned. The rule works pretty well concerning drinking, because that's difficult to disguise. Some teens, however, try to come in stoned, a condition that I'm fairly adept at spotting. One day I said to Kenny, obviously stoned, "Kenny, I think you're stoned, you know the rule." Said Kenny, "No, I'm not. What are you talking about?" At the start of the next session, Kenny displayed the stoned mannerisms, and I called him on it again—whereupon Kenny abruptly began talking and acting as unstoned as a judge. "Ha!" he said. "See, you're not as smart as you think you are!" (Now my rule is: You can't come to group if you're stoned or if you're *pretending* to be stoned.)

In a tight spot, an adolescent sometimes has this need to "get you," to demonstrate in one way or another or insist that you must be wrong. "Getting you" isn't bad or evil; it's just a defense. Teens often do feel terribly guilty about their transgressions. But they don't see any way out of them, so they have to defend them. Confronted with the evidence, your child is essentially finding another strategy to save himself from failing to cover up initially. This is why taking the time to gather information and be fairly certain of your facts puts you in a better position to be of real help to him if he needs it.

Catching Your Child in a Lie

You may have your own "gotcha" moment with your teen, when you point out to her you know for a fact that she's lying. My advice: Be careful.

Catching your child in a lie may not be difficult to do. However, there's a large risk factor involved in terms of your ongoing relationship. Your child loses face, she is humiliated, she becomes angry; perhaps she also must "take her punishment," if her parents decide to impose consequences. She will likely go to greater efforts in the future to keep all aspects of her life strictly a secret from you. Your job as a parent isn't to be a lie detector. As a therapist, I learned years ago that if my goal was never to be fooled or have one put over on me, I could succeed at that goal; what I wouldn't succeed at was ever having a meaningful interaction with the child I was seeing.

Most adolescents lie to their parents not to be dishonest but simply in order to be able to do what they want to do or to demonstrate their growing independence. It's an impulse that is developmentally appropriate, and it's really not the same as adult-type deceitfulness. Still, when you know your child hasn't told you the truth, you can feel terribly betrayed. You can also—and here's the real danger—feel so angry that you focus on the deception and fail to look beyond it to the issue that prompted it.

Control your emotions enough so that you can think about the possible problem behind the evidence and behind the lie. You may be extremely upset to find a packet of birth control pills in your daughter's room, but the important questions are whether she's having safe sex and whether she's having sex because she wants to and is ready. You may be terrified to see a clearly shoplifted item in a paper bag under your son's bed, but don't let your fear cause you to pass up the opportunity to find out more about why he shoplifted and what you might need to do to help him stop.

Teens sometimes have what seem to them legitimate reasons for lying. Occasionally, they *are* hiding something for a friend. Your daughter may have lied to you about where she was going because she was taking a friend to a Planned Parenthood clinic and she wanted to protect her friend's privacy. She may have stashed a pack of cigarettes in her backpack because her friend was about to be caught holding them. Covering for other children and trying to avoid bigger problems aren't great reasons for making up stories, but they're understandable reasons and they certainly shape the nature of any talk that might ensue between parent and child.

All this doesn't mean that you should never confront your teenager about known lies. But try to do so with words and a tone that convey your concern, your willingness to listen, and your wish to be helpful.

You might say, "I know you didn't sleep over at Alison's house last night. I know it's hard sometimes to talk about what's happening, but I would very much like to know what's going on."

Or "Josh, I came across this video game under your bed when I was cleaning your room. I know these are pretty expensive and I wonder how you got it. Can you tell me about that?"

Assume the attitude of requesting information; avoid immediate accusations or making a moral point. If you say, "It really disappoints me that you were so irresponsible and you lied to me," your child will decide you've already made up your mind about his behavior, and you won't hear anything further from him.

Putting Your Child on Notice

This goes along with going undercover, gathering information, building a case, and avoiding the "gotcha" confrontation. The aim is to let your child know that you have some concerns without blowing the situation by saying, "You're up to no good, aren't you!"

Adolescents are anything but stupid. Often they get away with incredible, not-so-good secrets because their parents never even let on that they *have* any suspicions. The parents don't let on because they don't know *how* to without precipitating a blowup and talk that goes nowhere. Mom or Dad says, "So, Jason, did you really spend the afternoon at the library like you said you were going to?" Jason replies, "You don't trust me, do you? You never trust me about anything, I hate you!" Jason is pulling a little power play. And children like Jason learn quickly that if they get upset and make accusations and create a big enough stink, their parents will back off, because parents don't like being in the middle of a big stink. In order to avoid one the next time they're concerned about something, those parents remain silent.

But you *do* have to say something. You must care enough to ask. Here's an example of how you can put your child on notice, or let your child know that you have your suspicions and they will have to be addressed sooner or later.

Eric, fourteen, had a weekly piano lesson (he'd been taking lessons for several years and was generally an avid student). The lesson was scheduled for four o'clock every Monday at the piano teacher's apartment, which was near Eric's school. One day his mother bumped into the piano teacher on the street, and the teacher mentioned that Eric often was showing up twenty or even thirty minutes late for his lesson.

Eric's mom wanted to know what Eric was doing after school that made him late. She considered spying (certainly one option), standing across the street when school let out one Monday and seeing where Eric went, but this was not practical given her job schedule. Deciding to double-check with the parents of some of Eric's friends, she called one mother and said, "I know Eric and Tony often hang out after school. Eric's always late for his piano lessons these days, and I'm a little concerned. Do you have any idea what the kids are doing, where they go?" She learned that Tony's mom also had suspicions about how her son spent some of his after-school hours and thought the boys were getting into pot.

Eric's mom talked to her son: "I ran into your piano teacher and she told me you're having trouble making your lessons on time. What's the problem there?"

Eric: "Oh, sometimes it takes me a while to get to her place, you know, like getting all my stuff together after school."

Mom: "Well, do we need to try to reschedule the time for your lesson?"

Eric: "No, no, that just happened a couple of times. It's okay."

Mom, in a sympathetic tone: "All right, we'll see how it goes. But you know me, I'm your mom, my mind runs wild and when I hear you're not at your lesson I start thinking you're out smoking dope with your friends or knocking over a liquor store or something."

Eric rolled his eyes and giggled. But Eric's mom had put him on notice, without saying, "You're in really big trouble if you're doing what I think you're doing!"

His mother checked in with the piano teacher one month later and learned that Eric had been on time the first two Mondays and late again the second two. Here's how the conversation went between mother and son:

Mom, turning herself in a little: "You know, I used to do stuff after school that my parents didn't know about. I wasn't always where I was supposed to be. But something that I'm concerned about with you, and I guess with anybody your age, is smoking pot. I know it doesn't seem like a big thing to you, but it can be, and I think it's something we ought to talk about."

Eric gave her the "You never trust me about anything!" response.

Mom: "Okay, maybe this isn't the best time to talk about it, you seem pretty upset. But I do want to talk about it later."

By saying, in effect, "I've put you on notice, we've marked the spot, we're coming back to this again in a little while," this parent was not allowing her teen to take control of the situation.

Often, a preteen or teen chooses one friend as a permanent "excuse": Your daughter's planning something she doesn't want you to know about, so she says she's going to Jessica's house. If your child has said three times in one week that she's going to Jessica's, mention that you've been meaning to call Jessica's mom about the PTA meeting next week or to talk about some plans for the upcoming school holiday fair. Again, without directly challenging your child, you've put her on notice that you're monitoring her activities and keeping track.

Parent and Child Problem Solving

Janice, sixteen, and her friend Kate jumped a subway turnstile one day, avoiding paying their fares, and were caught in the act by a transit police officer. The girls were fined $60 each. Janice mailed this amount in cash to the appropriate address. The money never reached its destination.

Janice's parents learned about this saga sometime after the criminal act itself, when Janice's dad answered a phone call from the transit police department and learned they were still waiting for their $60.

Janice's father put himself in his child's position and thought, *What would I be feeling if I got nabbed jumping a turnstile? What do I know about my child? Is she a delinquent? Does she jump turnstiles all the time because she thinks we live in a fascist government that doesn't deserve her fare? Nah, that's not my kid. Or, since she was with her best friend, madcap Kate, was she influenced to do something risky for a lark? Yes, that sounds reasonable.* Here's what he said to Janice: "Well, my dear, I learned about you jumping the subway turnstile, because the transit people called. I imagine that was a difficult moment, maybe a little scary. Of course, I'm not so crazy about you jumping turnstiles, but I'll bet you learned your lesson. And you have to pay a $60 fine." Janice, upset and embarrassed, told him she'd mailed in the money. Dad said, "Well, apparently it was lost. I understand you didn't feel comfortable enough to come to me and tell me what happened and say, 'Dad, could you write a check?' So what should we do? I prefer you not go to jail."

Daughter chuckled nervously at that last remark. Janice said she'd really like it if her father sent in a check and maybe she could repay him over time. Since she was already out of pocket $60, her dad said he'd settle for half.

That was a smart way this father talked about a situation that, really, was not painted in absolute black and white. It's easy for a parent to start off down a punitive road with a child who's committed a sin, then get stuck and feel compelled to maintain a stern front *(My child must not think I'm weak)*. Then it's easy to forget that sometimes it's important to acknowledge to a teen that you know her life is complicated, and sometimes there's an opportunity for generating new ideas (such as it's not smart to send cash through the mail).

A lot of drinking falls in this area. An adolescent has some drinks at a party and comes home looking woozy and slightly ill, and his parent flips out. Mom or Dad fears that the first beer or the first woozy evening means a child has started down a slippery slope toward utter destruction. Yes, the slopes are slippery, but teens hop off them all the time. And these are opportunities for you to listen and for your child, maybe, to learn.

It's also an opportunity for an adolescent, occasionally, to change her opinion about her parents. If you can have that conversation—listen first, withhold judgment, see what lessons can be learned—there's some blow struck for the possibility of a strengthened relationship between you and of mutual trust that will survive the troubling event. School-based mediation sessions, in which two children are required to explain their versions of a hostile incident, prove to be extremely useful not just because a particular dispute gets hashed out. The bigger gain is that teens come away imagining the possibility of joint problem solving. When you're able to problem-solve with your child—figuring out together better behaviors, reasonable controls or consequences, or where to find help—he can imagine the possibility of future communication with his parent. This is huge! Teens say to me all the time, "I can't believe it, I just had this amazing conversation with my mom. Who would have thought it?"

It's like: "Gee, I did something really rotten, and my mother didn't freak out and my father didn't ground me for life and they're still talking to me."

When You Need to Impose Consequences

Vincent, fifteen, was in trouble for lying about where he was two days in a row. As a consequence, his mother threw out all Vincent's rock CDs, removed the phone from his room, and said that for the remainder of the school year (about three months) he would not be allowed to go out in the evenings. Was this parent taking matters too far? That's a difficult question to answer without knowing some background. Maybe Vincent's mother and father had made a number of milder efforts to get their child's attention, and they didn't work. Maybe Vincent consistently ignored rules that had been discussed and established. Sometimes what seems like an extreme response to an adolescent's transgression makes sense, if it's part of an escalation of consequences over time in reaction to the child's increasingly secretive and dishonest behavior (an issue I talk about in a later chapter).

Here, I would make these general observations about the matter of imposing consequences.

Try to rein in the fear you have just experienced over your child's behavior.

Fear leads you, in a knee-jerk response, to mete out extreme and basically irrational punishments. "You're grounded for life" is so often a parent really saying, "I'm very, very scared, and so you can't leave the house until you're twenty-one." Often we need to make more unemotional decisions. You don't have to give the death penalty for every little misbehavior. Grounding, in particular, should be thought over carefully—because removing a child from the company of friends takes him out of a small community that offers him reinforcement for the positive aspects of his life. That's something he's probably not feeling much of at home in the aftermath of a transgression that set his parents off.

In addition to fear, anger can drive parents to issue extreme consequences. Julia, eighteen, came to group one day with the news that she'd been kicked out of the house. I asked what had precipitated that event.

Julia: "Well, I didn't come home for five days."

Me: "Yikes. That was pretty hard. Where were you?"

Julia: "I slept at friends' houses, and my parents were very upset."

Me: "Could you understand why they were very upset? They didn't know where you were."

Julia: "Oh, no, I called in all the time, they knew exactly where I was. They just didn't like it."

That was interesting. Julia had the common sense and enough responsibility to touch base at home and let her mom and dad know she was okay. But the background to this incident broadened the picture. Julia and her parents had been having many battles over her belief that she no longer had to gain her parent's okay over much of anything. Julia's attitude was, "I'm eighteen now. I can do what I want, and certainly you can't expect me to have a curfew anymore." After her five days with friends, her father erupted in fury and said, "Fine, do anything you want. You don't live here anymore."

After a brief cooling down, Julia was readmitted to her home, and parents and daughter took up a somewhat hostile truce. Here's an example of how imposing an extreme consequence in a fit of anger clouds the bigger issues at stake. Both camps—Julia and her parents—had right on their side, and what was necessary was relatively calm renegotiation of the ground rules. Her father might have said, "Look, we're glad you called and let us know where you were, that was good. We appreciate it. But we're not glad about you simply staying away from home for five days. That wasn't appropriate. So we need to talk about what's different now that you're eighteen and what's the same. You really can't live here and do anything you want. The curfew isn't about whether you're an adult or child, it's about respecting your parents and our being able to run a household."

Julia might have heard that argument.

Don't paint yourself into a corner.

Extreme consequences not only seem irrational to a child, they also can leave you, the parent, with no further wiggle room. When you threaten a child with a consequence that's essentially impossible to deliver or impose, either you must give way entirely or keep upping the ante.

Sixteen-year-old Patricia reported that she'd been grounded. "For how long?" I asked. "A year and a half," Patricia said. Her parents had kept doubling the grounding time for every little infraction of the rules, until they essentially decreed that their child was under house arrest until she reached the age of emancipation. Extreme consequences, of course, tend to make life miserable for everyone. I remember the first time I took away TV privileges from my son: "Okay, that's it, no more TV today, and if you do it again, no TV for two weeks." He did it again. And who knew how endless two weeks would feel like in the life of a thirteen-year-old—not to mention his father. He was horrible; I couldn't stand it. Don't threaten what you can't deliver.

Renege on a consequence you've set, if that's reasonable.

If you have painted yourself into a corner, revisit the consequence. You can say, "You know what, I'm being a dope about
this. Yeah, you did something you weren't supposed to do, but
my reaction wasn't appropriate. Let's talk this over again and
come up with something a little more humane."

That's what your child is thinking, anyway. And if you turn
yourself in in this way, you get great points with your adolescent, you really do. At the same time, you convey an important
lesson about perspective taking. We tend always to accuse our
children of not being able to step back, think things over, see
the bigger picture. Well, sometimes we don't, either. Your
child likes knowing that.

Whatever the infraction, remember that you can draw
boundaries and impose consequences, and still be forgiving.
It's like giving your child a suspended sentence. You're saying,
"You are charged, you're convicted, but you get another
chance. Here's salvation for you. I'm grounding you for the
next three weeks. However, if you demonstrate this or that,
you can be reinstated the last week."

Think about what's fair.

That is, what's fair from your child's perspective.

Screen time—use of the TV or the computer, including the
Internet, e-mail, and interactive video games—is a major cause
célèbre for many children. Not only do parents tend to think
their child is "wasting time," they also are often bothered by
what appears to be a child's secrecy over what he's up to on the
computer. He doesn't want you looking over his shoulder or
flips to another site when you wander by, and you're concerned.

Clearly, with some teens there may well be cause for a parent's worries and a need to monitor activities. But in the absence of a reasonable suspicion that a child is in trouble, it's critical to consider his point of view and how your controls on screen time seem to him. If you're reasonable, you're not likely to reach a point at which your teen says, "Reasonable is I can do whatever I want whenever I want, and I'm locking my door so you can't come in." That's usually a reaction to a parent's announcing, "You've got twenty minutes a day, and that's it."

Fourteen-year-old Paul and his parents fought constantly about screen time. Paul's parents knew he did a lot of instant messaging, they had been reading about the danger of kids getting into chat rooms, and they made a rule that Paul would be allowed one hour of electronic fun an evening. He said the rule wasn't fair, an hour meant only one TV program or only a little time on instant messenger when all his friends were on, and so forth. His parents were adamant, so Paul grudgingly complied. As it happened, one of Paul's favorite things during his one-hour screen time was to play a space mission video game. With such games, the player plays until the game is finished. Paul's parents, however, kept appearing at his bedroom door, announcing, "Okay, time's up, no more." Paul would say, "No, no, just let me finish this game." His parents insisted screen time was over, which to Paul seemed completely unfair and irrational.

Matters got worse. Paul started acting out; his father took the computer and the TV away. Paul sulked in his room, listening to the radio; his father removed the radio. This family came to therapy in a very bad state, with almost no useful communication happening.

Help your teen generate the consequences.

Give your child a chance to tell you what *he* thinks is fair.

Alice, sixteen, had a party in her house one Saturday evening when her parents were out for the night. She had been pestering her mom about how she desperately wanted to invite her friends over; mom and daughter had discussed the matter extensively; mom said no party. Alice had her little party anyway, which Alice's mother found out about the following week from another parent. It bothered her that not only had Alice gone against the rules but she had also taken great pains to keep it secret, hiding any evidences of the get-together. No empty pizza boxes, soda cans, or potato chip crumbs had been in sight. To Mom, it was sneaky business.

Alice's mother's first instinct was not to allow her daughter to attend the junior prom, a highlight of the year. She thought over that consequence—Alice had her dress and her date, and certainly it would, at the least, be humiliating for her to announce to the boy that she couldn't go to the dance. So here's what she said to Alice: "Look, you know I'm angry about you inviting your friends over when we decided you wouldn't. Any self-respecting parent would say you couldn't go to the prom as a consequence. But I know how important it is to you, I know you have the dress. So what else can we do to make sure you realize how serious your actions were? Something that hurts as much as taking away the prom. Maybe I should pick you up after school every day for the next month."

Alice: "No, no, not that!"

Alice thought for a while and then suggested she should not be allowed to go to the Fourth of July weekend party at her friend's parents' beach house that summer; she'd stay home and help her dad clean out the garage. Alice's mom said, "Sounds good to me."

Help your child generate the consequence. You may be surprised what she comes up with. Possibly it will be more onerous than anything you had in mind.

Let There Be No Shortage of Acknowledgment

It's a wonderful idea to let your adolescent know that when he obeys the rules, he's rewarded. Many parents feel that shouldn't be necessary: "Why should I reward my kid for doing the right thing? It's what he's supposed to do." "I shouldn't have to thank my child for calling me when she wants to stay out later, that's our rule." We just don't live in that kind of world anymore, and it's a good idea to reward good behavior. The reward doesn't have to be a used SUV. In fact, many adolescents are keenly aware of backhanded acknowledgments from their parents. They tell me, "You know, my folks are just buying me off." The reward can be, "I'm really proud of you," or a hug, or dinner out. Say, "Thanks for getting in on time. I know sometimes it's tough to make it back when you said you would." As parents, we're always coming down hard on "follow the rules, follow the rules." We seldom say, "Thanks for following the rules."

Acknowledge when a child is getting something right. I do that in therapy (of course, I have the luxury of not being that child's parent). I'll say, "You've really been under a lot of social pressure and you got suspended from school for a couple of weeks, and still you've managed to keep your grades up. Nice going."

When you acknowledge your child and say thanks, she feels appreciated, she feels trusted, and she's more inclined to cooperate the next time. Acknowledging a teen is so effective, and it doesn't cost anything.

Remember That Rules Work Both Ways

Parents must live up to their end of agreements also. But many have the idea that it doesn't go both ways (*I'm the father and he's the child and he has to live in fear of me, that's how it is*). That's tough for teens. Parents need to keep their end of the bargain, whatever it may be. If you tell your child she should be absolutely ready to leave her friend's house at nine o'clock because that's when you're coming to pick her up, and then you show up at nine-thirty, she feels a small betrayal.

This goes to the heart of agreements. Your teen thinks, *You expect me to do what I promise I'm going to do. I expect the same of you.*

Because of growing tension between parent and child during these years, there can develop a kind of teenage one-upping behavior: *Oh really, Mother, you think that's bad? Wait'll you see what I do next, that'll show you!* Pretty soon, that adolescent can get into serious acting out as a way of asserting herself, or sticking it to Mom and Dad.

But there can be several reasons for increasing secrecy. In the next chapter, I consider real trouble—dangerous secrets and what to do about them.

CHAPTER 6

Real Trouble

Dangerous Secrets and What to Do About Them

In this chapter, you'll read about several young teens and their families. Their experiences illustrate some ways adolescents can slip across the line into behaviors that are threatening to their health, safety, and well-being.

You'll see the initial signs and signals that point to something troublesome going on, and they will probably come as no great surprise to you. They include changes in sleeping or eating habits, shifts in general behavior, loss of interest in school and familiar friends, increasing secrecy about activities, increasing snappishness when Mom or Dad asks, "What's up? Everything okay?" Of course, these are among the signs that are occasionally part of the landscape of many adolescents' daily lives, as you well know after living with an adolescent for a while. One conclusion researchers have drawn from retracing the patterns of several teens prominently in the news for school shootings is that it's virtually impossible to create a reliable "profile" of a potential shooter—simply because so many kids fit that picture at one time or another; they're sullen, angry, depressed, feeling rejected.

So how can you know when your child's secretive behavior or demand for privacy reflects typical adolescent angst and when it's something more dangerous? My short answer is trust your instincts and your understanding of your child. Talk candidly to people, starting with your son or daughter. Gather intelligence. Learn what resources are available—there are many of them—to add to your insights or to begin to steer your teen onto a better track. And get help. Seeking help is anything but a sign of weakness. The fact is, you cannot possibly have all the information you need in order to take appropriate actions on your child's behalf from your perspective alone, and that's especially true if he or she seems to be engaging in destructive or potentially destructive activities.

At the same time, it's all too easy, all too human, to look the other way—and not out of apathy or a lack of concern or love. It's fear. Sometimes it's simply too frightening to acknowledge the possibility that a child may be in real trouble. So we say to ourselves, *I don't want to know. I don't want to believe. If I wait it out, maybe this whole bad situation will disappear.* Err on the side of caution. The consequence of asking and seeking help, and being mistaken (or overreacting), is generally a lot less than the consequence of not asking and not seeking help. Stepping in early usually does no great harm; stepping in late may be too late.

Parents who suspect that a child is in real trouble don't know the questions to ask, don't know what to do with any answers they might receive, and maybe aren't sure that the answers will be helpful. My suggestions in this chapter offer a road map through the approaches and options you have when your child needs your intervention and protection. The particulars I describe have been altered from real cases in order to preserve the anonymity of children and parents; they do, however, reflect common patterns that arise around these dangerous secrets.

Jack: A Boy Who Was Bullied

Jack was an eighth grader when I first met him and his family. He was a quick-witted boy who sometimes landed in trouble for his sassy remarks and jokey nature. His parents described him as a late bloomer. Jack was also small for his age.

Ginger and Rolly, Jack's parents, were both employed full-time, and the family had been sailing along comfortably until about a year earlier. That's when his parents first noticed changes in Jack's demeanor. He'd always been loud and a bit "out of control" at home, his mother said, teasing his older sister, fooling around. Now Jack was quiet and invisible for long periods. Often he returned home directly from school, went to his room, and stayed there until dinner. Rolly thought his son was just a little moody, typical young teen stuff. Ginger was more concerned, but her attempts to get Jack to clue her in went nowhere; Jack was evasive. At the end of the year, her concern deepened, because Jack's usually all B grades were now mostly.

But after a calm and uneventful summer—Jack returned to his old, familiar summer camp and seemed to have a fine time—Ginger was optimistic. Maybe Rolly was right and Jack had just gone through some "growing pains" last year. Once school started again, however, Jack plunged into gloom— silent, unreachable. At the first parent-teacher conference that fall, his teacher told Ginger and Rolly that Jack appeared sullen and withdrawn. She asked if everything was okay at home. Now both parents were worried.

That evening, they confronted Jack with their concerns about his dropping grades and his lack of interest in class. To their surprise, Jack—sounding sad and utterly hopeless— blurted out, "I hate school. I want to drop out." Ginger and

Rolly asked what they could do to help: Would he like a tutor for a while? Maybe Jack wanted his mom or dad at home more often? His response startled them: "I want to move away where nobody knows me." When his dad asked why, Jack replied, "Everyone hates me here."

But what came next was truly shocking to this mother and father. They offered the usual protests—"I'm sure that can't be true, I don't think everybody hates you"—until Jack lifted his shirt, revealing eight or nine deep bruises on his chest and lower rib cage. Some seemed new; some looked as though they'd been healing for a while. His parents literally gasped and demanded to know who was doing this. "Lots of kids," he said.

It had started the year before, Jack told them, when a new boy, Mike, made fun of him on the bus because he was so "puny." Jack attempted to fend off this verbal attack with a little joking sarcasm, which got him a punch in the stomach. The abuse continued the following day, and the next. Two or three other students, watching, seemed frightened at first, but then they too began to join in, pushing Jack around.

When his dad asked why he hadn't mentioned anything before, Jack was quiet, then he said Mike told him if any parents or teachers found out, he'd punch Jack until he was paralyzed, and he knew just where to hit him on the neck. Apparently Jack had been hoping against hope that his seventh grade tormentor wouldn't be on the same bus again this year. And Mike wasn't, but one of his old cronies was back in the rear of the bus and immediately gave Jack a sharp elbow to the ribs. A few days before Jack and his parents had their talk, three of the regular bus boys had ganged up on him after gym and shoved him into his locker. Some of the new bruises came from that incident.

After hearing Jack's story, his parents were outraged. Rolly's first response was to get the school principal's home phone number and call him immediately. Ginger thought they should meet with the teacher first thing in the morning. As his mother and father threw out these suggestions, Jack began to cry. He begged them not to say anything. In a small voice, he asked again, "Couldn't we move away somewhere?"

Jack calmed down a little after his dad assured him that nobody was going to punch him until he was paralyzed. It was agreed that they'd all talk to the school principal the next day. To everyone's relief, the principal was extremely responsive, and Jack and his parents left with a plan of action: The principal would take certain measures at school, including contacting the parents of the offending boys. Jack, the principal suggested, might like to have a few sessions with a local therapist, who conducted weekly group sessions with several children Jack's age who'd gone through similar torments. All this turned out to be enormously helpful to Jack, especially getting together with other kids to talk over their experiences. For a while, too, it was decided that Rolly would drive his son to school in the morning. By the end of eighth grade, Jack was feeling better; his grades improved and he was planning to return to his old summer camp.

This family's year-long struggle points to a common theme: Bullied children usually want to keep it a secret from their parents.

For one thing, the child feels there's nothing Mom or Dad can do to help; even worse, if he does tell some grown-up, then he's *really* in for it. In a typical scenario, the bully plants that seed: "If this gets out, you're double dead, I'll paralyze you." Children don't actually know *not* to take such threats at face value. When I work with a child who's being bullied, I sometimes ask, "Do you think this kid would actually break your arm, like he said?" And the child will answer, "Sure he will." A bullied child, or one who's being viciously teased, almost always wants to handle the situation alone, and not only because he's afraid of making life even more miserable for himself. It's simply inherently humiliating and embarrassing to be abused in these ways. The child is ashamed.

The reaction of Jack's parents was understandable. It's natural to want to rush in to bring a bullying situation to light and get higher authorities involved in order to put a stop to it. Conversely, some parents urge a child to "ignore those kids" or "just walk away or sit somewhere else"; some—especially fathers—suggest that the child "stand up to these guys, don't let yourself get pushed around." Somewhere between these extremes lies the better solution.

Is my child being bullied?

Given a child's reluctance to reveal the problem, that's often a hard question to answer. Some parents say, "I think my son is getting a little roughed up by a couple of kids, but I've asked him if everything's okay and he says, 'Fine.'" Don't let it drop. Take these steps:

Notice specific signs of trouble. In addition to unusually withdrawn or worried-looking behavior, and bruises, such as Jack displayed, other clues that a child may be receiving abusive treatment from other children include:

- He has a hard time leaving for school each day.

- What seemed like beginning-of-the-term nervousness doesn't get better as time goes on.

- His clothes or bookbag look torn, dirtied, or disarrayed when he returns home.

- He often complains of not feeling well in the morning and says maybe he should stay home that day.

Let your child know that you're on to something. That might mean saying, "Son, I'm concerned by some things I've noticed . . . ," and mention the repeated headaches, the dirtied clothing, or the bruises. "Sometimes we get into circumstances that are hard to control or talk about, like getting hit. Has that sort of thing happened to you?" Or, if that's too hot, "Has that ever happened to any of your friends?"

Give him a vote of confidence. If he reveals that he's being pushed around by another child, ask, "What have you tried so far? Can you avoid this kid? Have you talked to him? Talked to your teacher? And how has that worked?"

Let him know that you know he's gone to bat for himself. Acknowledge that he hasn't simply been a helpless, pushed-around wuss. Maybe what he tried didn't produce results, but he has, in fact, attempted to solve his problem on his own.

Create an atmosphere of collaboration. Say, "Okay, let's see if we can figure out some other ways to deal with this. Would you like me to call this boy's parents? Would you like me to talk to your teacher? Should we go together to talk to her?"

Even if a child wants to handle the situation alone, he does need to know that his parents are aware, are behind him, and aren't going to leave him to the mercy of the bully if he can't protect himself. Bullying situations often do need parents to step in.

Is my child abusing other kids?

It's a little harder to figure out if your child is a bully, especially once he's in the preteen and teen years. If you have suspicions that your child may be abusive, ask yourself the following questions:

Where can I gain more intelligence? Maybe your child's friends drop some clues that he likes to rough kids up. Other parents might hear about or observe incidents. There's nothing wrong with calling a teacher and asking, "Has my son's name ever come up in terms of difficult behaviors in school?"

Does my child always seem angry? It's in the nature of bullies to act out an impulse to control others or to express their anger. Of course, many teens are angry sometimes, which doesn't make them bullies. But if you observe a striking shift in that direction, if the anger is persistent and excessive, be concerned.

Have there been scenes of physical, inappropriate anger? Such as by punching his hand through the sheetrock in his bedroom?

What language does my child use? A bully tends to be intolerant and judgmental. He doesn't say, "I don't like that guy." He says, "I hate that creep."

Surveys indicate that as many as 30 percent of children are bullies and/or victims. Both bullies and victims need help—not only for the sake of their own healthy growth and development. Bystanders—the other 70 percent of the peer population—are often deeply upset and affected by observing bullying incidents. This is nasty behavior to be a part of, even if only as a witness.

WORKING WITH YOUR CHILD'S SCHOOL

Parents are often uncertain about if, when, and how to involve the school in helping a child who's caught up in a bullying or bad teasing situation, or is being painfully ostracized. Maybe you're not quite sure what's going on and need more information. Maybe you've learned enough from your child to believe it's time to take an action. In either case, here are some suggestions.

Befriend the school.

Studies show that when children reach the junior high and high school years, parents tend to drift away from the school setting. If that's the case for you, get back in touch. Find out who does what and who can talk to you. That may be the guidance counselor, the principal, the assistant principal, the teacher in charge of attendance or disciplining, or a caring teacher.

The school nurse, if your child's school has one, may be a source of information. The honorable way for a child to get out of school—when he's having trouble coping on a rough day, or is coming down from some bad pot smoking, or has been cornered in the bathroom by a couple of kids who threaten to beat him up—is to appear in the nurse's office and say, "I don't feel well, I need to go home, please call my mom to come and get me." Girls tend to be more successful at this approach, partly because adults believe girls are more emotional and psychosomatic than boys, partly because it's possible to use menstrual complaints on a regular basis.

But many school nurses are shrewd about why a child might be turning to her for deliverance. If he's regularly showing up with a stomachache on Fridays and asking to be dismissed early, for example, a nurse might conclude that since the medical literature mentions no gastrointesti-nal maladies that strike only on Fridays and since that's the only day without extracurricular school activities, the child is desperate to avoid the bus ride home.

Try to find out with whom your child has a special connection.

Ask him, "Is there any teacher you especially like?" Some-times, though not always, you can pry this information out of him. If your teen claims to have no favorite teacher, try to think of one you know—from school conferences or other functions—who seems to like *him*. That might be a good individual for you to contact.

Make yourself heard.

My rule is, call anyone in the school who'll talk to you. It re-ally is appropriate to ask questions. In my work with schools, I've observed that teachers by and large are ecstatic when a parent calls and says, "I'm worried about my son Jonathan . . ." Teachers feel they can ally themselves with the parent to help the child, instead of sensing, as so often is the case, that they and the parents are somewhat adversarial.

At the same time, most of these individuals are doing fifteen things at once, so you as a parent must get yourself noticed. You might say, "I know you're terribly busy, but I really want to sit down with you soon and share my concerns about what's going on with Jonathan."

Explore options.

It's up to the school to decide what action, if any, will be taken against a bullying child. He or she might be suspended, or required to perform certain services to avoid suspension. That child's parents usually are required to meet with the teacher or principal.

Many schools have bullying prevention programs, but parents typically aren't aware of them. So ask, "Is there anything in place that can help my child in this situation?" You may learn that certain classes have curriculum discussing the issue. Some schools do mediation—getting involved children to sit down and talk (which sometimes is effective and sometimes isn't).

Most bullying incidents take place outside the classroom and beyond the watchful eyes of teachers, in schoolyards, in locker rooms, and on buses. A school mental health professional—social worker or school psychologist—may be of help by suggesting specific measures to end the behavior. Then it's usually up to that individual to coordinate the effort with the teachers, sports coaches, and/or bus personnel.

> ### Establish some form of ongoing communication.
>
> If you and your child make the decision that you will establish connection with his school in these various ways, think about how to carry that on. Maybe you and his teacher or the school mental health professional can agree on a once-a-week phone call or exchange of e-mails. Maybe you can schedule an extra conference. Just let it be known that you plan to keep on top of the situation and will be asking for updates on how the helpful procedures are working.

Marcy: An Internet Romance

Marcy, an only child, lived with her parents—both lawyers—in an upscale urban neighborhood. Like many privileged kids, she was nicely equipped with a TV, stereo, and state-of-the-art personal computer in her bedroom. Marcy was a decent student, had many friends, and enjoyed sports. Physically mature for an eighth grader, she nevertheless seemed to have little interest in boys, or so her parents thought.

In February, they began noticing changes in Marcy's behavior. Mainly, she stayed closeted in her room in the evenings. Sarah and Will, her mother and father, weren't terribly concerned, because their daughter was constantly at her computer. In fact, they'd previously suggested that maybe she was spending too much time with her friends and too little on her schoolwork, so they were pleased that she seemed to have taken those words to heart.

Then the secretive behaviors became more striking. Thirteen-year-old Marcy would barely walk in the front door before she was off to her room and logging on. She stayed up until all hours, and some mornings she appeared exhausted. When Will and Sarah questioned her, Marcy said she was doing research for a school project. "Oh, what kind of paper are you writing?" Will asked. "Just some stuff for science," Marcy replied.

Will decided to speak more pointedly one evening. "Look, sweetheart, your mom and I are a little worried about your being on the computer all the time. We've read stuff about the kind of chat rooms and whatnot kids can get into, and so we'd like to know more about what you're doing. When I asked you about this school research and you were so vague, that made us get a little more nervous, to tell you the truth." Marcy blew up, with typical adolescent arguments: "You never believe me, you don't trust me, it's my business."

That confrontation, combined with the other signs they'd been observing for a number of weeks, persuaded Will and Sarah to take an action that made them uncomfortable but that they felt was necessary. An associate in their law office who was knowledgeable about computers helped them figure out Marcy's password. After she had left for school one morning, they opened her e-mail and saw hundreds of messages from the same person—Jason, a boy (so he said) who apparently lived a few hours away. Besides affectionate talk and some lewd language, the most recent e-mails included instructions on how Marcy could catch a train to his town. Her replies indicated that she had already selected a date a few weeks in the future to "make my break and find you and be with you."

That evening, Will and Sarah told Marcy what they had done and what they had found. She was outraged, then complained bitterly that they never let her be grown up or do anything. The arguments became heated, until finally parents and daughter reached a compromise: Marcy would have no further contact with Jason until they checked him out in some way. "Look," said her father, "maybe he's an okay kid for you to keep in touch with, although you will not go running off to meet with him secretly. But we need to find out first whether he's really the age he says he is or if he's an older man who's trying to solicit young girls, and even if he really is a teenager, we need to know if he's in any trouble."

To Marcy, although she still objected, this was tolerable. At least her mom and dad weren't clamping down on the computer entirely.

Will and Sarah actually weren't sure how to proceed but decided to ask at their local police department if it was possible to investigate Jason. After that, they told their daughter, it might be time to sit down together and come up with some rules about the computer and maybe they all should have a session or two with a family therapist. "E-mailing a boy you haven't met is one thing, which doesn't thrill me," said Sarah, "but planning to sneak off to meet him scares the life out of me."

Marcy's communication with an unknown boy was one of three kinds of secretive computer activity that may point to real trouble and that, rightly, raise parents' alarm bells. In addition to chat room correspondence and e-mailing unknown "romantic" partners, as in her case, parents worry about a child accessing pornographic material and making or receiving threats.

In any such situation, here's the rule of thumb: If you have a reasonable suspicion about what your teen is doing on the computer—because she shuts the screen down any time you're in the vicinity, or is tapping away at odd hours of the night, or is evasive when you question her—you must bring up the subject with her. This is a "need to know." Ideally, as I've said before, you will have warned her (though I prefer to think of it as "training") ahead of time to expect a degree of vigilance on your part: "As your mom and dad, we might sometimes want to know exactly what you're up to on the computer, because we need to make sure you're all right."

Is my child making a romantic connection over the computer?

Invading her e-mail when she's not there is certainly one way to find out. A better way is to ask her and hope that she'll tell you after you let her know why you're concerned. When you learn she is carrying on a secret correspondence:

Set immediate limits if you have reason to think the contact is dangerous. It's dangerous if, as in Marcy's case, your child is planning an in-person rendezvous with an unknown person. You and she really have no way of knowing if the correspondent is actually a forty-six-year-old man, or a kid who's fronting for a forty-six-year-old man, or just a teenage creep. And it's dangerous if the computer conversation is highly and explicitly sexual, or if it's clear your child has not revealed her own real age.

As with Marcy, the first limit needs to be, "You can't have further contact with this person until at least we find out more about him."

Marcy's dad's comment to his daughter was wise: You can't go running off to meet him, but it might be all right for you to remain in touch. Determine if the boy is an appropriate person and then make a decision on that basis. Maybe you can suggest that a meeting can take place, but it will be in your home with you present. If he's not an appropriate person, stop the behavior entirely. Say, "It's dangerous for you to communicate with him in any way. This isn't a safe way to meet someone."

Ask the police to investigate. Most police departments have Internet investigation divisions. Possibly the local police division can run a check on the person your child is communicating with.

Rethink the use of the computer, together with your child. "I can't trust you, you're off the computer for good" is a tactic that will backfire in one way or another. However, especially with a younger teen, it's worthwhile to ask, "What would you rather do on the computer than go to these chat rooms? Let's do some searches, maybe we can buy some new software." Divert her attention elsewhere by trying to substitute another, healthier use of the computer to which she's become so attached.

Then, "You need to be taking part in other things besides hanging on the computer. You used to talk about horseback riding lessons, would you like to think about that now? Maybe we can arrange it." You're conveying to your child this message: You can't do nothing, and you can't do nothing except be on the computer day and night, so what else seems remotely appealing to you?

A consultation with a family therapist, such as Marcy's parents suggested, might be a good idea. It's important to know if a child is chatting with boys or young men online because she's eager, or perhaps desperate, for connection and doesn't have better outlets for finding it.

Is my child downloading pornographic or violent materials?

The father of one preteen said to me, "You know, I think my son is secretly looking at porn, but I don't want to open that can of worms. He's way too young to be into that stuff, anyway, so probably he's not. If he is, well, it's not really dangerous. When I was his age, I used to go to the library and pore through the *National Geographic* magazines, trying to find those pictures of naked people." To which I say, "Find out for sure what your child is looking at. You need to know."

Is it dangerous? Images that depict degrading, controlling, and/or painful sexual acts, or children and adults engaging in sex, are not healthy for your child to see under any circumstances. Images that depict how the human body looks without clothes, it can be argued, are not dangerous for a child to see. There is a difference between what's pornographic and what's erotic. However, what you do and don't want your child to access on the Internet must depend at least in part on your personal values. If you have religious, spiritual, or other objections to your child's viewing nude and/or sexual images of any sort, that's something you should express. Aim to be protective without overreacting, because a teen inevitably will respond to the overreaction ("That's dumb, Mom. You're so behind the times.") and ignore the protective argument.

Ultimately, you're the arbiter, and the trick is to be able to flex your muscles without pushing your adolescent to be more devious. So a good way to proceed if you suspect your child is secretly looking at porn:

Put him on the alert, without implying you'll be trying to catch him doing something "bad." Say, "I'm going to ask to see what you're watching because I may not approve of some of it, and maybe we will have to get some monitoring software." Find and install software controls that actually work. Tell your child, "I know you think this is dumb and I'm treating you like a baby, but I need to do this because it's my responsibility as a parent."

Engage your child in a little discussion about what you consider a problem and she doesn't. Software controls aren't especially useful with an older teen. However, you can gain some traction by sharing your thoughts and asking for hers: "Why do you think I'm upset about your looking at this stuff? Why would I not want you to be able to download porn? Are you interested in these sites to keep up with your friends, or to be popular? Okay, if I believe there's too much of this coming through, what are we going to do about that?"

Occasionally watch teen-oriented TV with your child and talk about it.

Some children don't actually know what pornography is, or what images might be considered lewd. Viewing rock videos on MTV or VH1, it's hard to tell where to draw the line. The following kind of conversation might be useful:

Mom: "I think this performance is a little much, what do you think?"

Son: "Uh, don't watch this, okay?"

Mom: "Why don't you want me to watch?"

Son: "Well, you're not going to understand."

Mom: "What am I not going to understand? That that woman is almost naked, or they're gyrating around like they're having sex? And she's wearing a dog collar and a leash?"

Son: "Mom, that's so gross!"

Mom: "Well, why are you watching if it's so gross?"

Put some pressure on your child to think about all this.

Adolescents are smart. If your child is intent on outwitting you, he will; he'll download porn sites on a friend's computer. There's no real way to stop that, but at least you've taken a stand in your own home, by explaining why you don't condone and don't like this kind of viewing. Then your child gets to consider values you do hold. When I meet with an adolescent and his parents in a therapy session, and mom or dad voices an opinion—about *anything*, whether it's rock videos or clothing styles or fast foods—the teen is invariably surprised. He's surprised because he didn't realize his parents actually held opinions, because he hadn't heard them expressed before.

Has my child made or received threats over the computer?

Boys with Internet secrets tend to be those who are sending or receiving threats. E-mailing threats happens from home to home, but frequently the behavior comes to light in school, when one child threatens another over the school library computer and gets caught. In the wake of instances of school violence, schools rightly take such matters extremely seriously these days. If your child happens to be involved in such activity, on either end, you may know nothing about it until the school launches an investigation. Here's what is in your power to do:

Educate your child. Marcus, twelve, was instant-messaging his friend Jake when his dad happened to walk by and read over his shoulder. Marcus had typed in the news that he was going to get a gun and blow Jake's head off. Marcus's father was appalled; Marcus said they were just kidding around.

Boys do make threats as jokes. Go into a chat room after a humiliating loss by the football team, and you will likely read postings that sound alarming: "Boy, that third down call was the pits, somebody should just point a gun at that guy's head and put him out of his misery . . . Yeah, or break his legs." This is sort of coin-of-the-realm talk; to a twelve-year-old it's just making a strong point. Marcus thinks, *I typed a little message, I'm not going to really* do *anything. What's the big deal?*

Certainly, inform your child about how it *is* a big deal if you stumble across him making computer threats. Even if you have no reason to believe he's engaging in such behavior, inform him anyway, so he won't get into it in the first place. Here's what kids need to understand:

- You must be careful about what you say on the Internet. You cannot threaten people for fun, because you can wind up in a lot of trouble.

- Schools can suspend or expel threateners. Even if you threaten another student from one home computer to another, you still may be suspended—just as you can be suspended for starting a fight at the bus stop, though the bus stop isn't technically school property.

- The person you're threatening can call the police on you, because some Internet behaviors are illegal.

Don't assume that a threat your child has received is innocuous and don't assume there's nothing you can do. If Jake is scared that Marcus really means it about blowing his head off, he has legal recourse. Marcus could be charged with an assault, which by definition is any action by person A that causes person B to believe he's in danger. Assaults, including threats, are as valid now in virtual reality as in physical reality. In addition, an individual making an Internet threat across state lines can be charged with a felony.

Call the police and ask what resources are available to you. You may be advised to download and copy the threatening messages; you may be told what charges you are legally able to bring against the threatener.

WHEN AND HOW TO INVOLVE THE POLICE IN A TEEN'S SECRETIVE BEHAVIOR

I've discussed some times and ways you might want to talk to your local police in order to check out someone your child is in touch with over the computer. The more difficult police contact—in fact, the hardest for a parent—comes from the decision to report one's adolescent for possibly criminal behavior. I urge parents: If you have any suspicions at all about what your child is into—an expensive new DVD player appears in his bedroom; strange-looking envelopes or packages are coming in or going out of the house—talk to him. Tell him your worst fears. Tell him you're scared to death that he's involved in illegal activities. When parents ignore or deny their suspicions, it's all the more likely there'll be a knock at the door one day, with an officer saying, "Is your son home? We have reason to believe he's been involved in a robbery."

But contacting the police is sometimes a good idea or a necessary move.

Call to obtain information.

You think your teen might be dealing drugs, but you have no idea what to do next. Inform yourself. You can usually phone a local police precinct and speak to the desk officer, or phone the juvenile court service and ask questions without leaving your name. Ask, "What happens to a child who is selling ecstasy? What kind of crime is that, what penalties are involved?" You may be pressed to reveal why you're interested. Say, "I'm just asking a general question." Then you may decide to obtain advice from a lawyer on how to proceed.

Call if you are frightened for your own or others' safety.

Some parents truly believe they are in danger of physical harm from their adolescents. A parent might say, "My kid shoved me hard against the wall, and usually I'd say he'd never hurt me in a million years, but this time there was a look in his eyes that scared me. I can always kind of joke around with him when he's angry, but this time I couldn't." That may require calling the police.

Call if you know your teen is involved in behaviors that are threatening to his life or others' lives, if the danger is imminent, and if all other avenues of intervention are unavailable or have been ineffectual.

Andy: Abusing Drugs

Andy, his younger brother Rick, and their parents George and Judy were a close family, enjoying many activities together during the early years—kayaking, hiking, and rock climbing were favorites.

Andy had always been an excellent student until, about three weeks into ninth grade, he suddenly lost interest in school. He missed the bus frequently in the mornings because he had a hard time getting up. Throughout that year it seemed to his parents as though Andy was just "coasting." They questioned him, tried to jolly him out of his increasingly sullen moods, but Andy said he just wasn't into school anymore and they should leave him alone. Rick, then in sixth grade, was doing fine, although the close relationship between the brothers began to deteriorate. Andy often seemed angry at Rick; on one occasion, he punched him in the face hard enough for Rick to require stitches over his eye. But the more his parents tried to talk to Andy or be helpful, the more he rebuffed them, spending almost all his time with his friends, or alone.

As tenth grade began, Judy and George hoped matters would turn around for their son and he'd get off to a good start. He'd been a pretty good soccer player when he was younger, and they urged him to go out for the team. Andy replied that soccer was for jerks. "Of course it went through our minds that he might be using drugs," Judy said much later, when Andy was in treatment. "That's what you worry about. But I didn't want to believe anything like that. And I didn't know how to find out." She did, once, ask her son, "sort of tentatively," she said, "if he was smoking pot or something." Andy replied, "Don't be stupid, Mom." The turning point came when, six weeks into the fall term, Judy received a call from Andy's school one Friday afternoon, asking why Andy had not been in classes the previous week. Judy was shocked and panicked. She was certain he'd boarded the bus every morning—so where did he go?

While Andy was away for the weekend at a friend's house, Judy and George looked around his room. In his T-shirt drawer, they found a baggie with something that looked like marijuana, a pipe, incense, matches, and room deodorizer. When Andy returned home, his parents confronted him, telling him what they had heard from the school and what they'd found in his room. Andy's response: Sure, he smoked pot, he said, all his friends smoked and he had no intention of stopping. His parents told Andy he absolutely would need to stop. Andy said, "No way."

George and Judy were at a loss. Overreacting frightened

them, but so did not doing anything. The bottom line was that they weren't really sure how much of a problem Andy was having. Did all his friends smoke pot? Did smoking marijuana mean he was addicted?

So they told Andy he was grounded for the next four weekends, and then George got to work on the Internet hunting up information. Based on what he found, George and Judy decided that their first step should be to get Andy evaluated at a local treatment center. Andy, of course, resisted but finally agreed after they offered to shorten the time he was grounded.

What they learned was bad news: Andy had been involved in frequent marijuana smoking, as well as cocaine and ecstasy use. He smoked not only in the afternoons and weekends but also every day before school. After the evaluation, Andy was referred to group sessions with other teens, which he attended on and off for that year, but it was no magic turnaround. In the early summer before his junior year, he stayed out many nights, often appearing back home seemingly stoned or spacey. At that time, Judy and George made the decision to send Andy away, against his will, to a three-month residential treatment program. Returning home, with a supportive treatment plan, Andy struggled to finish high school, then took courses at a community college for a year before finally deciding that he would stop drugging and attend college full-time.

The experience of these two parents in recognizing, facing, and coping with their son's drug use illustrates common themes in this form of secretive adolescent behavior.

A child begins to show signs of drug abuse over time, and Andy's progression was fairly typical: slumping grades, lack of interest in school, irresponsible behavior, increasing absence from the home, and eventually downright withdrawn behavior. Some children become more depressed as time goes on.

But here is an important point to understand: Despite all the news about pot, cocaine, and ecstasy, the drug of choice for many adolescents is still alcohol. Sometimes that flies under the radar because alcohol is often so readily available in the home, because smart kids learn how to dodge their parents, and because parents are often in denial. Mom or dad will catch a child once and rationalize, "Well, okay, I got drunk a couple times myself when I was his age, no big deal." The parent fails to spot a pattern of behavior.

A surprisingly large number of parents don't know that their adolescents are alcohol abusers. One father happened to glance at his daughter's yearbook after it had been signed by her friends. To his shock, almost all the messages related to substance abuse: "I'll never forget getting shit-faced with you on the beach . . . Hope we have many more Rolling Rock moments in our future . . . Sorry about getting smashed and smashing your fender." (And this father was remembering, *Wait a minute, she told me the fender got nicked when she was parked at the mall.*)

Of course, substance abuse is behavior that an adolescent keeps secret. So how can you know what's going on?

Is my child abusing drugs?

Question your teen about the peer atmosphere he travels in. Ask him what other kids are doing, because he's much more likely to talk about them than about himself. Ask if there's beer drinking at the parties, if lots of kids are into pot.

Observe his friends. Maybe talk to those children's parents. If his six best friends seem to drink a lot or smoke pot, if they show up at odd hours looking or sounding out of it, if you hear for a fact that one kid is always getting grounded because his dad caught him again with beer, you can bet that's an issue for your child. He will not be spending time with that group unless he's into similar activities himself.

Consider your family history. Heredity is one criterion for addiction. If there are alcoholics in the family, that doesn't mean a child will inherit alcoholism. It does mean the probability is higher.

Ask yourself what you already know that you need to be careful about. What might become an issue for your child? If it's alcoholism, adolescence is the time it becomes an issue. Then it's reasonable to say, "Given what we know, let's keep our eyes peeled." If there are alcoholics in the family and you see that a bottle of vodka is missing from the cabinet and you wonder if your child took it, you need to be worried; if there are no alcoholics in the family, you still need to be worried, but at a different level.

Check things out neutrally at home. Watch the liquor cabinet, the wine rack. Take note of a constant use of breath fresheners or room deodorizers.

Once you have any suspicions, put your teen on notice. Starting out with an accusation—"I know you're smoking dope!"—is usually a bad idea. But do let him know that you have observed behaviors that worry you, that you will be watching what he's up to, and that if your concerns grow, something will be done.

Seek out professional help and support. As in Andy's case, that might start with a substance abuse evaluation.

Whether the drug of choice is pot, cocaine, ecstasy, or alcohol, your child needs help. Parents sometimes tell an adolescent, "Get your act together, pull yourself up by the bootstraps." The environment, unfortunately, does little to support a teen in that effort, or makes it simply too difficult even if he has the willpower and determination. The truth is, pulling a child back from substance abuse often isn't possible for parents to accomplish on their own.

For one thing, as time goes on, a child's addiction may be getting worse (he has greater need for the substances), just as his developmental desire to be independent is growing, and that's a deadly combination. So he becomes even more skilled at jumping through the cracks for the purpose of maintaining his secretive behaviors and meeting his need to take drugs. That, sadly, is when a parent can conclude the child is sort of a lost cause and give up on all aspects of parenting. In addition, adolescents with addictive problems require special handling. They need greater structure, more confrontation and, almost always, participation in AA-like programs that will call them to be accountable.

For these reasons, I believe it's useful to approach addictive behavior as a disease, because that mind-set can prompt parents to accept the enormity of the task in front of them. If your child was diagnosed with diabetes, you wouldn't say, "Well, you better think more carefully about your sugar intake." You'd say: "Take the pill, take the shots. This isn't negotiable."

A SUBSTANCE ABUSE EVALUATION: HOW TO OBTAIN ONE AND WHAT TO EXPECT

If you're worried that your child is regularly using alcohol or other drugs, if he is stonewalling your attempts to question him or intervene, and if you are not certain how seriously he's involved, you should get him—by hook or crook or bribery—to an evaluation. You need to know. Here's how to start that process and what to expect.

Begin with your child's doctor.

Substance abuse is such a common problem among adolescents that pediatricians and family doctors usually have referral sources to offer. Tell that doctor, "I don't know if my kid is on drugs or not, but there have been some signs indicating that he is, and I'm worried. Where can I take him?"

Ask your child's school.

Call the school nurse, the principal, or the guidance counselor. Generally, that individual will accept such an inquiry without it plunging your child into further difficulties or garnering him a black mark. Many schools work with substance abuse programs, or at least are aware of them. They have referral sources.

Contact your local mental health association.

Most evaluation services are funded by the state or locality, but usually for adolescents there exists some form of community mental health center that can provide you with information, if not service. These may be referred to as community service boards, behavioral health authorities, or child guidance centers.

The facilities differ dramatically from community to community. Some have walk-in evaluation services; with others, it's necessary to be placed on a waiting list, or to be referred by a physician.

Check with AA.

If you know someone associated with the Alcoholics Anonymous structure, that individual may have useful information
about where your child can be evaluated.

Look in the phone book.

If all other avenues fail, try to find a private practitioner
who lists himself or herself in the phone book as a spe-
cialist in substance abuse evaluation.

What to Expect from a Substance Abuse Evaluation

Usually the evaluation involves a first interview, sometimes with the parents present and sometimes only with
the child. Your child will be questioned, and a skilled
interviewer will elicit the information of what drugs he has
used, with what frequency, and so on. Some of that information may be held confidential between child and interviewer. Depending on the facility you use, your child may
also be administered blood and urine tests.

Based on what's learned in the evaluation, the center or
practitioner will make recommendations for treatment. That
might include individual counseling, and usually attendance
at meetings (AA, Alateen, Nar-Anon). Most treatments do
have a built-in meeting program, so this isn't an alien connection. There are many available groups, and it shouldn't
be too difficult to find one with some appeal to your adolescent. Some are specifically designed for substance-abusing
teens, which tend to be a little more confrontational than
general groups, or groups for adolescents who are not there
primarily for drug abuse.

*   *   *

Andy's progress through and eventually out of drug abuse occupied more than four years of his and his parents' lives. He felt in retrospect that his several months in a residential facility had been helpful. However, coming back to "the real world," as he said later, was a hard transition. His struggle wasn't over yet.

Residential programs differ from one another. Some have a Christian orientation; some operate by tough love principles. Some are organized around Outward Bound activities; some are nurturing. Substance abuse evaluation centers usually have information on such programs. But any parent who makes the difficult decision to elect this form of help needs to anticipate what goes with it, including what must come afterward.

For many parents there's a feeling of relief, as well as great sadness, when they send their child away. They're happy when he returns; they assume he's better. And often, the child is better, because he's received a structure that supports what he's trying to do for himself. That's just why and when parents can become less vigilant themselves. And that can be a painful mistake. The child at this crossroads in conquering substance abuse might think this way: *I'm making a promise that I intend to keep, to end destructive behaviors. As long as I have a structure that supports me in keeping that promise—talks to me about it every day, gives me consequences when I waver—then I'll probably be able to keep the promise, and I'll feel good about myself. But if I have trouble keeping it, am I strong enough to maintain my promise myself, without support?*

The answer is, usually not.

Parents need to do their part in supporting the child to keep his promises—starting immediately, as soon as he comes back, at the time he is most motivated to keep that structure going. This is both difficult and a pain in the neck, because it's trying for the parents and annoying to the adolescent. But parents must speak candidly: "Look, you know and we know that this is a disease. If you were diabetic, we would probably say every evening, did you take your insulin today? Not because we think you're a dummy, but because the consequences of your forgetting are too great. So let's you and us come to an agreement about how we can best monitor you and remind you of what you need to be doing, without us making you feel like we're treating you as if you were five years old."

When a teen says, "I'll never do it again," you don't say, "Oh, okay." You say, "Oh, okay, and if you do it again, here's what's going to happen." In the following chapter, "In the Wake of a Storm," I look at ways parents can provide the structure—in the home, every day—a child needs to keep his promise to get off drugs or alcohol. Quite often, he'll continue to need outside help as well.

HOW TO FIND A MENTAL HEALTH PRACTITIONER

Once any threat of immediate danger is past, the child who's been flirting with real trouble in some of the ways I discussed will usually benefit from counseling with a mental health practitioner, who may be a psychologist, psychiatrist, or social worker. Here's what to look for.

Find someone who has expertise in the area of your child's difficulty.

You may come up with a name or two by word of mouth, from other parents or friends who have used professional services. Some communities have referral services through the local mental health center. Ministers often have referral suggestions. Or contact one of the professional associations in your state, such as the psychiatric society, the psychological society, the association of social workers, and the licensed professional counselors association. Most have Web sites now.

Make an appointment to meet the individual you've decided upon. Direct, pointed questions are appropriate. Ask about credentials. Is he or she a psychologist (Ph.D. or Psy.D.), social worker (M.S.W.), or a professional counselor (M.A. or M.Ed.)? If you have questions, say, "I'm dense about these things. Could you tell me a little about what kind of training that involves?" Any practitioner should be willing to talk about his or her qualifications and how he or she works.

Look for board certifications that show that the practitioner you have selected has a commitment to professional development. Most states now have requirements for continuing medical education in some form.

Yes, finding this kind of help is a nuisance. It takes time and it's upsetting. But consider: If you were having plastic surgery, which had the potential for being disfiguring as well as helpful, you'd be very careful in selecting a surgeon. When your teen's psychological well-being is involved, the decision is just as delicate; one size cannot fit all.

Find someone who is a good fit for your child.

You want a practitioner who is qualified, but just having credentials is not enough. A perfectly well-trained individual may simply not click with your son or daughter. Then not only is he or she not helpful, he or she is making matters worse. This may destroy the credibility of any future therapeutic contacts. "Yuck," your child says, "you made me go to that drippy social worker before, I'll never do that again."

This is the tricky part: How do you know whether the therapist is the right match for your child?

First, a good practitioner should tell you if he or she and your child don't seem to be hitting it off. As a clinician, I sometimes see a teen who arrives determined *not* to allow any rapport to grow between us. I do have some tricks up my sleeve to suggest that he might find it useful to talk to me, and I'll certainly try those approaches. But sooner or later, if we haven't made progress I'm going to say, "It's not really helpful for you to see me."

Second, listen to your child. Some kids will say, "Dr. Smith is an idiot, she's stupid." "Stupid," of course, often means, "I don't want to do this." On the other hand, maybe Dr. Smith really is not on your child's wavelength. It's appropriate for you, as the parent, to request another meeting with the therapist, just to gauge the lay of the land. Then, possibly you'll agree with your daughter: Dr. Smith *is* a little stupid.

Give the process some time.

The good/bad fit can't be determined after one session. Usually, I say to my client's parents, "Give me four weeks. Make your child come for four weeks, and if after that time you're still *making* her come, she might want to see somebody else."

Shop around.

If your child and the practitioner are not clicking, look further. When parents say to me, "We'd like to come in and see you, and we're interviewing a couple of other people too," I'm delighted—because a good fit is important for the therapist too.

Of course, in the managed care context in which we live, shopping around is a pain in the neck: You arranged to have sessions with a psychologist authorized by your insurance company; your child says, "I don't like her, I want to see somebody else"; you must now contact your insurance company again and ask who else is on the list, and so on and so on. Nevertheless, it's essential that you have confidence in the therapist and your child has some rapport with him or her.

Finding help should not be an adversarial prospect. You do not want to say to your teen, "We're going to find you a therapist whether you like him or not, damn it, and you're going to go." You do want to say, "Look, there's a problem going on here and let's find the best person to help, and the best person is one that you and I agree is going to work. If this one didn't, I care about you and I'm concerned enough that we'll keep looking."

Jen: The Girl Who Cut Herself

Jen, fifteen and in tenth grade, lived with her mother, Nina, and younger sister, Tracy. Always a pert and attractive girl, and a fairly popular one, Jen had gained a few pounds over the summer and was "filling out," as her mother saw it. Jen herself seemed preoccupied with her body, poking at her waist and complaining about "all this blubber I'm getting." When she failed to make the cheerleading squad at school that fall, she was initially inconsolable, then seemingly uninterested. Nina tried to talk to her daughter: "You must be disappointed, honey, are you?" and "Were there a lot of kids trying out this term?" Jen replied, "I'm fat and ugly, that's why I didn't get it, okay?"

Over the next three months, a lot changed for Jen, in ways that concerned her mother. Nina didn't hear the names of Jen's friends, or see around the house any of the girls she'd come to know. There were many phone calls for Jen, who always took them in the privacy of her room. Several new kids were now part of her life, and these girls seemed a bit more "wild" to Nina. They dressed with a lot of exposed skin; they had multiple piercings. And Nina found it harder to keep track of Jen, who was gone most of the time every weekend. Mother and daughter had one confrontation on a Saturday night, when Nina said she really didn't approve of an outfit Jen was wearing, and Jen blew up in anger and ran out the door.

From then on, communication between them dried up to a trickle. Nina wasn't sure what to do, or even how she felt about this new scene. On the one hand, she thought she should set more boundaries for her daughter, like insisting that she stay home some evenings and spend time with her and Tracy. On the other hand, seeing Jen looking more upbeat was better than the gloomy, depressed stretch at the beginning of the school year.

Nina said much later, "I guess I wanted to keep my head in the sand. I told myself this was a teenage phase she was going through." Two events caused her to "wake up," she said. Putting laundry away in Jen's room one Sunday evening, she saw on her computer table a folded note that had come open.

It said, "Jen, I'm waiting for you," and gave a phone number though no name. Taped to the note was a condom. At that moment, Jen came in and shouted, "Excuse me, what are you doing in here?" Mom showed her the note and asked, "What is this? What does this mean?" Jen replied that it was none of her business and left the house.

Nina sat down to think, alarm bells going off in her head. Was her daughter having sex with boys who simply left their phone numbers? Was Jen even going to come back home that night? She did, much later; Nina tried to give her a hug, but Jen just pulled away and went into her room, closing the door.

The second wake-up event occurred the following day. Late in the afternoon, at her office, Nina received a call from Sarah, a girl who'd been one of Jen's close friends a year ago, one of the old crowd. Sarah said she'd asked her mom to find the phone number for her, she was sorry for bothering Nina at work, but there was something she thought Nina should know. Sarah said, "Some of us are getting worried about Jen, because she's hanging out with kind of weird guys and she's been cutting herself."

Nina was now fairly panicked. Rather than approach her daughter directly—"I believed, truly, she might just run off for good"—Nina crept into Jen's room when she was asleep that night and gently pulled up the sleeves on her long-sleeved nightshirt. She saw three straight cuts across the outside of one arm. The cuts seemed a few days old.

The following morning, she was waiting at the kitchen table with a pot of coffee when Jen breezed through to pick up a quick bite before heading off to school. Nina told her that both of them were staying home that day; they would sit down here and have a talk. They did, for a couple of hours. Jen looked suddenly, Nina said later, "like a deflated balloon. More sad and frightened than angry and combative, like she had been for all these months." Jen admitted to sleeping with two boys, because they made her feel "special." She said she cut herself just to feel better. Mother and daughter cried together.

They decided to talk to a therapist. Nina asked a friend at work for some references; Jen knew the name of someone a friend was seeing. Mother and daughter met twice with a therapist, and one outcome of those meetings surprised Nina: Jen said she really wanted to spend more time with her mother. Then Jen began regular appointments with a clinical psychologist.

Nina's and Jen's story highlights one form of secretive behavior that's especially worrisome for parents of adolescents: how a child copes with apparently unbearable levels of stress.

There is no particular profile for children—they are primarily girls—who cut themselves. Some seem very pulled together, popular girls who earn good grades. Neither is there one outstanding explanation for the behavior. Occasionally, it takes the form almost of a fad. A girl in one middle school cut herself badly, in a genuine suicide attempt; within a week, nine other girls in the school had cut themselves too, literally walking through the halls with blood running down their arms, entering classrooms holding their arms up. The initial incident proved socially contagious.

Whatever the reason, cutting is an act that, understandably, makes parents absolutely hysterical. A parent's first thought is, *My God, she wants to die!* responding to the stereotype of slitting one's wrists, the classic way of killing yourself. Obviously, it's critical to know if an adolescent is thinking about suicide. At the same time, most girls who cut are not suicidal. Here's what is so difficult for parents to understand: The girl who cuts herself feels a sense of relief afterward. She might explain, "I don't want to die. When I hurt myself like that, it calms me down." Some girls say, "I just want to feel something. Before, I felt numb; now at least I know I'm here. Look, I made blood." This is an action she can take to produce a specific result she needs. Sometimes it's a desire to get attention. Often it's not, and the child goes to great lengths to hide it, by making cuts on the inner or upper arms, the backs of thighs—a place that can be covered by clothing. It's somewhat like the child who burns himself intentionally with a cigarette; he may be disturbed, depressed, stressed out, but he doesn't intend to kill himself.

Drawing blood—which is often done with a paper clip, a dull razor, a pen, not with the sharpest knife—is usually a way for the child to control the intense anxieties she experiences. For some, cutting is a stress management technique that passes once they reduce or resolve their stress, or develop better ways of managing it.

But adolescents have other reactions to and ways of dealing with stressful feelings. Depression—when the teen isolates himself, just wants to be left alone in his room—is often a sign that everything in his life is too painful to handle at the moment. Internalizing depression of that nature is what we adults most commonly experience—we feel low, we can't sleep or we sleep too much, we don't want to talk to anyone. There are, however, forms of adolescent depression that are externalizing, involving agitated, acting-out, risky behaviors. One boy said that when he was feeling depressed, "when it's like I'm disappearing," he'd do something dangerous, "because it wakes me up." Another teen often would drink six beers and then take off on his motorcycle, in the rain.

Although it's not entirely accurate to lump together a number of behaviors—such as cutting, depressed symptoms, indulging in risky activities—it is clear that these adolescents are not happy. They're not coping well. They just don't feel good about their lives at the moment. They're managing stress in unhealthy ways.

Parents are pretty sensitive to whether their kids are happy or not. And yes, a teen might grow out of it, but there are too many bad possibilities, too many ways a child can hurt himself, to take the chance of waiting it out. If you think your child isn't happy, intervene.

Is my child seriously anxious or seriously depressed?

The first point to make about Jen's and Nina's story: If your child's friend calls to tell you something about your son or daughter ("We're sort of worried about Jen . . . ," "I don't know if I should be saying this, but Tom seems really down lately . . ."), take his or her concerns seriously. That friend has already violated the adolescent code of silence by talking to a parent.

Monitor your child's behaviors more carefully. The key to spotting depression is this: The child is not herself. It can be argued, of course, that once kids get to be teenagers and enter the age of great biological and social upheaval, they're never themselves. But if you're at all concerned, pay attention to how your child is acting and consider whether it's extreme or just not like her. Look for dramatic changes: mood fluctuations, oversleeping, undersleeping, overeating, undereating, nervousness, anxiousness, or agitated, acting-out, hostile, or angry behaviors. Anything that's not characteristic of your child and that lasts for a month or more is a symptom of depression.

A girl who's cutting herself might suddenly be wearing nothing but long-sleeved shirts and long pants or never taking off her sweater even when the room is hot. Maybe you're having to replace a box of Band-Aids once a month. These are tipoffs.

Make note of the children your teen is spending time with. As I noted, if an adolescent's four best buddies are regular pot smokers and beer drinkers, chances are he is too. If her new friends are a bunch of scrawny, anorexic-looking kids, there's probably a reason she prefers being around them.

Don't take "Leave me alone" as an answer. You say, "Is everything okay?" Your adolescent says, "Leave me alone." That should be the beginning of a conversation, not the end of one. Quiet, withdrawn children often don't sufficiently stir parents to action, which is understandable. It's the squeaky wheel that gets the oil. But even, or maybe especially, if your child isn't making any noises, trust your instincts that something's up. Try to be home more often. Take him out to dinner.

And keep a conversation going. You have to try to get through to your teen. You don't have the luxury not to try. You're not allowed to give up, even if you experience defeat upon defeat.

Talk a little about what you've observed or about yourself. Do not come across as if you're accusing your child of something: "Are you depressed? You're depressed, aren't you? You're acting very strangely and I can't make sense of it, there's got to be something wrong, tell me what it is." That's not an invitation to communicate. What might be an invitation is, "You know, you seem very quiet lately. I don't mean to pry, but I'm concerned that you might be kind of down about stuff. Certainly I get that way sometimes, and you've probably noticed that. Sometimes it's helpful to talk. I know maybe you don't want to talk, but just keep me posted."

Deciding that your child will communicate with you or else is the quintessence of how *not* to approach the moody teen situation. The secret is, your child is always communicating with you—maybe not in your terms or in a language you understand, but he is saying something with his behavior, including disappearing into his room for hours at a time. Don't make your self-esteem contingent upon how well you're getting through, because whether or not your child makes you feel good about yourself as a parent is secondary. First in importance is what's actually good for him.

Get a doctor's evaluation. When the signs and signals are adding up, and you feel you're not getting a straight answer about anything from your child, obtain an outside evaluation. Start with someone your child considers "safe," who might be the pediatrician or the gynecologist who's now seeing your daughter. Pediatricians and gynecologists who work with teens observe a lot of depressed or dangerous behavior.

Obviously, a psychologist or social worker is a good idea, but that can seem like a drastic step to both parent and teen ("You haven't taken a shower in a week, you're sleeping a lot, let's go see a shrink"). But you can say, "You know, you haven't had a checkup in a long time, I'd like you to go back to Dr. Warren and get one. And ask about whether you should have a flu shot this fall." Then tip off the doctor: "I'm concerned about Misty, she seems kind of off her feed, I'm worried she's depressed. So I'm going to get her over for a checkup." Start that ball rolling.

Ask your child, "Do you ever think about hurting yourself?" This might not be your lead question, clearly. But don't be afraid to ask it if you are genuinely worried about what your child might do. Most suicide attempts are what we call silent attempts, never discovered. Adults, and even a child's friends, don't find out about it. The child might take a lot of aspirin, but not enough, and wake up the next morning feeling better. The point is, she should never have to get that far.

It's common for a parent to believe, "Oooh, I'd better not ask my kid if he's thinking about hurting himself or killing himself, because that might put the idea in his head." To which

I reply, "Over years of working with adolescents, it has never once been the case that after I said to a child, 'Are you thinking about hurting yourself?' the child has answered, 'Well, no, I wasn't, but now that you mention it, it sounds like a good idea.'" We get too scared to talk about some issues. Don't be too scared. If you're concerned that your teen might hurt herself, ask her.

Find a good listener for your teen. All situations are different, but the child who's anxious or depressed often also feels incredibly lonely. It's a highly internal experience. The adolescent senses, *There's no one I can tell, no one who can help, I just have to suffer with this myself.* Girls who cut themselves, for example, believe they can't have a conversation about it with anyone who won't freak out. If she tells her mom, she'll hear, "What are you doing!?" and she just wants to cut herself some more, because nobody understands.

For any child who's depressed or anxious, knowing that he or she has an ally and someone who'll try to understand is tremendously important. In addition, a trained listener—a medical doctor, psychologist, psychiatrist, social worker, school counselor—can help the teen, and his or her parents, see what might be underlying issues, or what the child's needs are. A symptom doesn't always mean the same thing. The symptom is the starting point, not the end point. Yes, you have to stop the behavior, but how you go about stopping it may be related to why it's there.

Dangerous secrets can develop out of emotions or experiences a child finds overwhelming. Some children are simply less resilient or more sensitive than most of their peers. Some feel the normal stresses of adolescence more keenly, in the same way some people can distinguish temperature better than others. Sometimes slipping into real trouble is just bad luck, when a child is the wrong kid in the wrong place at the wrong time. That might be a school environment in which, for one reason or another, his classmates decide not to like him. A trauma— any unique, difficult event, such as the death of a parent, or long-ago abuse by a neighbor—or a dramatic change in surroundings—such as moving to a new town or the birth of a sibling—can suddenly throw the developmental trajectory off, and a teen heads down a different path.

For parents, such passages are not pleasant, and certainly not easy. But keep in mind these general thoughts about dangerous secrets and what to do about them.

Face Up to It

It's terribly hard to face up to the possibility that an adolescent is in real trouble. I said at the beginning of this chapter that denial and avoidance often grow out of fear. We think something's not right, but it's too frightening to find out that's true.

But facing up to it is also a nuisance and an embarrassment: *Oh, God, I got a call from the school. Now I have to go down there, I have to follow up, I have to do something and where do I start?* And then: *What does this say about me, that my child is now in trouble? Am I going to be blamed for whatever is going on? Am I going to hear that my kid wouldn't be in this mess if I'd done a better job, given her more structure, not come from an alcoholic family myself?* What parent wants to open himself or herself up to all that?

Wrestling with these human, understandable emotions, it's tempting to avoid or delay or close one's eyes and just hope that tomorrow will be a better day. But a teen's dangerous secrets need attention, sooner rather than later.

Because Your Child Kept a Bad Secret from You Doesn't Mean You Failed

You're not a dreadful parent because your adolescent didn't tell you what she was up to or didn't turn to you for help. Mom says, "I'm so disappointed, crushed, and hurt that Valerie didn't come to me. I thought we could talk about anything." However, teens can't always distinguish between the good secrets and the bad secrets, the "normal" secrets and the dangerous secrets. Valerie's perspective on her activities might have been, *I have this neat relationship with this guy on the Internet, he's someone I can talk to, there's no sex, nothing bad going on.* Valerie's mom finds out and thinks, *She didn't want to tell me, I must be a terrible mother.*

Feeling like a bad parent leads to overreacting or underreacting, and either sends the message to a teen that Mom or Dad doesn't want to understand anything. But showing that you're willing to try to understand is the beginning of real support.

When your child's dangerous secret has come into the open, he's not necessarily going to be thrilled and thankful over being "found out" and helped. He may storm and rage and indicate how much he hates you and everything you're doing, which again can add to a parent's sense of misery and even failure. Try hard not to take those outbursts personally; recognize them as transient.

If your child is struggling, it doesn't mean that you're not doing the right thing.

When It Comes to Truly Dangerous Secrets, Professional Help Is Often Necessary

In the box on page 156, I presented some suggestions on how to find professional help for your child. *Getting to* that step, however, is what's so daunting for so many. The words "therapy" or "professional help" usually strike dread into the hearts of parents and teens alike. But as the experiences of the children and parents I've described demonstrate, real trouble—or the possibility of real trouble—calls for a marshalling of all available troops. An adolescent's dangerously secretive behavior is usually more than parents can deal with on their own. So I offer these further thoughts to assuage the dread—which exists partly because Mom, Dad, and adolescent suspect they're in for a long, long haul.

In fact, professional help can take place in a circumscribed and effective way, and in stages. For example, I often consider myself a psychological physician for a family. Just as you don't visit your medical doctor once a week, but go in for checkups occasionally or when something hurts or is broken, it's possible to establish an off-and-on relationship with a mental health practitioner. I see many teens in sort of waves of dysfunction. Christopher's mother tells me, "Chris is doing well now, his grades are picking up, he doesn't want to come in for sessions anymore." I say, "Good, call me if things change." Perhaps six months later I might hear, "Well, it's all coming unglued. I just lost my job and that's been a stress on everybody, and Chris broke up with his girlfriend, and I'd like to bring him in and see what's going on."

This is fine; it's like getting a booster shot. The kind of long-term, psychodynamic therapy with which we have become familiar from movies such as *Good Will Hunting* isn't the norm. A skilled practitioner—a trained listener—can make a productive intervention with a family or with an adolescent in a couple of sessions. And then you have built up a little rapport with someone who knows you if and when you need him or her again.

Parents say, "There is no way in hell I could get my kid to see a therapist." First, I suggest, try to create an alliance with your teen. Don't make therapy the overriding issue, and don't make it punishment. You might simply say, "You seem not to be your usual self, you spend a lot of time doing things you didn't used to do before, and that concerns me. When you tell me not to worry, it doesn't make me stop worrying. And so I'm wondering whether you'd consider going to somebody to talk about this. Even just for us to find out that it's nothing major. I'll get Chinese takeout afterward."

You don't have to sell your child on professional help; you just have to get her there. After that, it's the practitioner's job to make a connection with your child. I tell a parent, "Just bring Sally here and then it's kind of up to me."

Most kids resist going. Most good therapists acknowledge that fact at the outset, by saying something like, "How do you feel about being here? If I were you, I wouldn't want to be here either. Frankly, I'm not always so happy to be here myself. So let's start from there. We're stuck, your folks are plunking down the money, let's kill half an hour doing something that might be useful, tell me a little about yourself."

It works. Sometimes, the relief factor kicks in; what the adolescent anticipated as a hideous ordeal turns out to be, at least, less than hideous.

In your initial meeting with the practitioner, it's perfectly appropriate to set some behavioral goals, if that makes sense to you. Maybe Sally's mother says, "I'm concerned that Sally has become so withdrawn, doesn't talk to any other kids, and I'd just like to see her make one or two friends by the end of the school year." This suggests a future to aim at, and provides, sometimes, an opportunity for midcourse corrections. If it's November and Sally's mom hopes her daughter will have some friends by May, what will that look like in February? Has Sally reached out to one person? Joined an extracurricular activity? Can she be further encouraged to do so?

After that, trust the practitioner to be able to engage your child and work with her, and don't micromanage the process. That's difficult, because it's very scary if she seems to be in real trouble. But you did your homework, you found useful resources, you shopped around if necessary, you asked for help. One of the most difficult messages I convey to parents is this: Do your best, do what you believe is right for your child, and maybe she will be ready to take advantage of it or maybe not. Part of it is up to her.

Let Your Child Know
What You Expect to Happen Next

The strategies in this chapter have to do mostly with recognizing when a teen's secretive behavior is disguising real trouble. You may not be able to predict it, but you need to be sensitive enough to see the signs when they arise and respond to them with appropriate forms of help. Ideally, that's the beginning of the end of dangerous behaviors on the adolescent's part. But it also must be the beginning of the beginning for what comes next, which is going to be a little different from what went before.

During this transition stage of parenting, and especially after a time of trouble, mothers and fathers can easily become caught in the cycle of telling children what they *don't* want them to do. The smarter and, in fact, necessary message is: "This is what we want you to do, and this is what that will look like, and here's how we, your parents, are going to support you as you do what we want you to do."

For many adolescents, maybe most, the world is very confusing. They don't know what to expect from it. It's your job to say, "Here's what you can expect from me, sweetheart." That includes defining behaviors, setting limits, and imposing consequences after a teen has betrayed a parent's trust or has begun to pull back from dangerous behaviors—which I turn to in the following chapter.

CHAPTER 7

In the Wake of a Storm

Trusting Your Child Again,
Repairing Your Relationship

Suppose you find out that your fourteen-year-old has been secretly spending time in a boyfriend's apartment after school, though you and she discussed at length the reasons you think that's a really bad idea. Or you were summoned to the local police precinct to retrieve your sixteen-year-old after she and two friends were smoking pot on the street and were picked up by a cruising patrol car. Or your seventeen-year-old has begun treatment for substance abuse, and you suspect he's not sticking to the program. You wonder what your proper role or next move should be. You believe you must "punish" the disturbing behavior in some way, in order to convince your child that he or she would be wise to give it up and in order to demonstrate your concern. When he or she was younger, you had some strategies that weren't too difficult to enforce—a time-out, a "go to your room and think about what you should do differently," "no TV for tonight." Now it's not so clear.

In fact, one or two of the old consequences are still workable. Sending a teen to his room isn't one of them, because that's where he probably prefers to be anyway; however, no TV, or restriction of access to the phone or computer, might still be pretty effective. But especially in the wake of a storm—when your teen has already been "caught in the act"—it's necessary to think about the overall structure you provide him and how that might need to be adjusted.

Parents whose adolescent is getting into trouble of one sort or another are often given the suggestion—by the pediatrician, by a teacher or counselor at school, by a mental health practitioner—that the child needs more structure. But the parents don't necessarily know what that means or how they are to produce it. Structure encompasses rules, expectations of appropriate behavior, limits, consequences for poor behavior, consistent routines, rewards and praise, expressions of love, and demonstrations of support—all the influences that allow a child during these turbulent transition years to develop his identity and enjoy his freedom, while still feeling secure, guided, and contained by caring adults.

But often it is exactly in the wake of a storm that providing more structure—reexamining the whole matter—is most difficult. That's when a parent is terrified for a child's safety, or incensed that he went out and did the very thing he agreed he wouldn't do, or worn down from dealing with secretive behaviors that have become more entrenched. Typically one of two reactions is common.

Mom and Dad become rigid, scary, punitive, and overcontrolling. They say to their child, in effect, "You lied to us, you let us down, you're not going anywhere or doing anything for the next four years."

Or Mom and Dad become lenient and essentially give up on him. They say, in effect, "Okay, we got you help, we tried everything, nothing worked, you're seventeen, you're on your own. You win."

Either reaction can have a disastrous effect, which is usually to push a teen back into further secrecy and even more unacceptable activities. When parents crack the whip and seem to lay down a life sentence, it's just too difficult for the child to change for the better. He hears the message, "We'll never trust you again, so don't even bother trying to get back in our good graces." When parents cut the child loose, he loses his bearings entirely. He hears, "It's not worth all this time and energy on our part to fight for your well-being, we're not your parents anymore."

There's a better way—really, the only way to give your child what he most needs after he's been racking up mistakes. Create a way back. Show him how he can honorably return to the fold. That might start out by acknowledging that you're not feeling too optimistic at the moment and that it will be hard—not impossible, but hard—to trust him again; it's going to take work and some sacrifice on his part.

It will also involve work and sacrifice on your part, which is why imposing consequences and setting limits is something you'd probably prefer to put off until another time. Talking yourself out of it is easy to do; in fact, it's the most human inclination in the world. For one thing, no one's in the mood to re-play a bad scene, or sort of hold it up to the light of day afterward and consider what new rules, if any, ought to be put in place. The mother of fifteen-year-old Tim expressed this notion succinctly: "I found out totally by accident, because I happened to be driving by, that Tim was hanging out in the park in the evening and drinking beer. This was when he said he was going to a basketball game at school. I talked to him when he got home, and the talk turned into a screaming match and I couldn't sleep the whole night. The next day I thought, Thank God that's over with and I never want to go through that again."

There are any number of ways to talk yourself out of taking action. Do any of the following arguments sound familiar?

We're going on vacation next week. I'll wait until we get back.

School's just starting. I want her to get off on the right foot, now isn't the time to make a big issue about how she's been breaking curfews.

The semester is almost over, his grades are looking good. I don't want to rock the boat with a lot of rules and regulations.

But putting off the inevitable, or what should be the inevitable, has two negative consequences. First, it's like the sword of Damocles, constantly hanging over you. Second, your adolescent is likely to feel that Mom and Dad aren't paying attention, or maybe they don't care, so he can pretty much do what he wants.

Here are several ways to go about promoting change for the better and important considerations when you're trying to restore a trusting relationship between you and your child.

Five Parental Steps to Restoring Trust

In Chapter 5, I offered general ideas on talking to your child about what behaviors you expect from her and what happens if she ignores or abuses them. That included setting up ground rules in advance, listening to her arguments, leaving room for negotiation, helping her generate her own consequences and, when necessary, putting her on notice that you have observed some things that concern you and they will have to be addressed sooner or later. Behind all such discussions, you're saying, "I want you to enjoy your freedom, maintain your privacy, and make your own decisions. At the same time I will be meeting my responsibilities to watch out for you and to guide you."

In this chapter, I'm assuming that matters have gotten a little more out of hand. Your teen has shown by her actions, maybe on three or four occasions in a row, that you were overly optimistic in thinking she was in control of herself. She gave lip service to mutually agreed-upon ground rules and then ignored them. Maybe your child must pull himself back from substance abuse, and you know he's not sticking to the program. The mood is not one of relatively amiable give-and-take as I described earlier (though the give-and-take element shouldn't be missing entirely). Here's what to do.

Step 1: Calmly explain what behaviors must change.

I emphasize the "calm" aspect, because when confronting a teen in the aftermath of repeated or serious bad behavior, typically you're angry. Then it's natural to lash out, forgetting that the goal of this unpleasant confrontation is to teach a child to take charge of himself in better ways. Saying "I'm so mad at you, so disappointed in you, I don't see how I can ever forgive this" only teaches a child to be hopeless. Don't let your emotions rule the day.

Neither is it effective to say, "All right, we're going to start having some new rules around here, mister, you just wait and see." The rules and expectations must be specific and spelled out. It is perfectly appropriate to say, "What you did is bad, and in the future we will expect you to stop breaking curfews/drinking beer/cutting school/smoking pot/lying to us about where you're going/having parties when we're out." Or whatever it is he must change.

End by saying, "You can restore our confidence in you. It may be a long road, but let's consider now exactly how you can go about this."

Step 2: Outline a plan of improvement, which includes consequences.

You might begin by asking for your child's input: "So, what's going to be different from now on? What do you think appropriate consequences should be? What can we do to help things go better for you in the future?" This sounds good in theory—and it is good—but it doesn't always work in practice. Maybe he answers "I dunno" to each question. When your child is contributing nothing to the plan but staring at you—or at the ceiling—in mute resistance, offer your own suggestions until you activate a response.

Adolescents are deliciously contrary. In therapy, some decide to defeat the process by simply not speaking. Here's a tactic I find useful, which can be just as effective between parent and child. I say to the silent teen sitting before me, "I don't blame you for not saying anything. I think I'd be very guarded if I were you, and I think you have reason to be that. But we've got to make progress here, and since you're not talking, I'm going to assume that if you don't respond to something I say, that means it's all right. So first, if it's okay with you we'll meet once a week."

The child says nothing. I continue: "Okay, fine, we settled that. Now let's talk a little about what you're going to do in between those times. You're going to have to restrict your behavior, and probably a good way to do that over the next week is by going home directly from school instead of hanging out with your friends in the park, because that's where you've been getting into trouble. Does that sound okay?"

The child still says nothing. "Good," I say, "we're getting somewhere. Next, I think it would be a smart idea to have your parents come in about two weeks from now, and we'll talk about . . ."

Finally, the child speaks: "No!" Now we have a little dialogue going.

It really is useful to prod your teen into involvement with the plan for his improvement, because he's then more likely to abide by it and because he recognizes that you're trying to treat him somewhat like an adult.

What the consequences should be depend on the situation and the individuals; however, any should be presented as: "Here's what you can do to demonstrate responsibility and to earn our trust again. You can pay for the repairs to the car/respond to a curfew that's one hour earlier than it has been/baby-sit your little sister this weekend/realize that for the next month, we're not going to leave you home alone for more than an hour at a time/realize that you will not be allowed to use the car for two months." Probably, you won't want to slap him with ten such onerous challenges at once, but two or three might sound right. In the event of continued offenses on his part, you can let him know that the list might be added onto.

Grounding, of course, is a powerful consequence, and one that—as I mentioned earlier—should be weighed carefully, because it's often only in the company of his friends that an adolescent feels positive and good about himself. They are the people who validate his existence. Now, in the wake of a serious betrayal of your trust, grounding might be the most appropriate way to get across how serious *you* are about what's been happening: "Until we're sure you're able to start making the changes we've talked about, you won't be able to go out with your friends on the weekends. We'll set this for the next two months, and we'll see what happens."

If your teen regularly receives a weekly allowance from you, consider reducing that for a specified period of time. Or make it a daily allowance, giving her just enough to let her join her friends for a soda after school. (A survey by the Columbia University National Center on Addiction and Substance Abuse found that teenagers who have $25 or more a week in spending money are nearly twice as likely as those with less to smoke, drink, and use illegal drugs, and more than twice as likely to get drunk. If any such behaviors are part of his problem, you can mention this to your child, by way of demonstrating your determination to help him change for the better.)

Reducing TV, computer, video games, and telephone time is an option at your disposal.

Whatever the consequences, present them within a time frame. There is a light at the end of the tunnel, and the tunnel doesn't stretch into the child's middle age. An exercise coach I knew used to say, "Your goal is to be more fit today than you were yesterday." To your teen, you're saying, "We want you to be more in control today than you were yesterday. And we feel confident that two weeks from today, or four weeks from today, if you follow the path we've outlined together, you'll be in greatly better shape."

Nobody—you or he—should have any uncertainty about what behaviors have to change and what happens if they don't. In fact, sometimes it's useful to write all this down, making a list of rules and consequences and formalizing the agreement between you.

Step 3: Enforce the rules and consequences.

Once you lay out goals, consequences, milestones, and rules, be really good about enforcing them. As long as they're sensible, justifiable, and/or attainable, you must not let them fall by the wayside or go back on them, because doing so gives your teen the impression that none of this was very important. Possibly there's room for negotiation—when things are looking better—but there's no room for breaking a rule.

Step 4: Restore privileges as progress is made.

When the rules are consistently followed, restrictions can be gradually removed. Here's where some negotiation can come in. If your child has religiously demonstrated his willingness to abide by the rules—he's home for dinner every night, he's reading a book instead of watching TV, he's showing you his schoolwork—you may feel all right about making an adjustment; maybe a two-month grounding can be reduced to six weeks. The aim is for your child to return to a "normal" level of independence when he's ready, not sooner—but not much later, either.

Step 5: Celebrate progress as you continue to monitor behavior.

Living under what seems to him like severe restrictions is not a pleasant thing for an adolescent. It really is work and sacrifice. He needs regular pats on the back, so he feels good about himself and so he's encouraged to do even better in the future. Tell him you're really pleased with the progress he's making. Tell him you appreciated it that he was home for dinner every night, or in whatever ways he's shown greater levels of self-control and responsibility. Tell him you knew he could do it.

Tailoring the Steps to Fit Your Teen and You

Again, as in all aspects of Stage 2 parenting, one size does not fit all. Know your child and what is most likely to be effective in producing change for the better. Although in general, rigid, overcontrolling parenting backfires—either by causing a surly, resentful teen to become more so, or by fracturing a willing child's motivation—sometimes the tough love approach works. A parent might say, "It's a battle of wills, me against my kid, I've got to lay down the law," and with that child, at that time, laying down the law is actually what's needed. What might be completely dogmatic and unreasonable for one child may be okay for another, at least for a while. Some children do require a steelier structure, although ideally they will also be allowed some degree of input into what the structure looks like.

All this has to do with a child's unique needs, with his temperament or personality, with the influence of peers, and with the nature of the parent child/relationship. And it has to do with how you discuss your expectations for him.

When I was about age nine, I had a diary with a lock and key. I lost the key. So I went back to the store where the diary came from and stole another key. My mother learned of this crime, and I knew instantly that she was crushed and saddened by what I had done. Her response was interesting and, I realized—much later—smart; she insisted I return the key to the manager of the store. This idea seemed dreadful to me. "Couldn't I just leave the key back on the counter where I got it, right next to another diary? No one would ever know," I pleaded. "No," she said, "that's not the point. The point is, you can't steal, and there are consequences if you do." Me: "But I could get in real trouble." Mom: "Yes, you could." I did return the key to the store manager, and thankfully, I avoided real trouble. And I never shoplifted anything again, not because of that embarrassing confession to the manager but because I had only to remember the look on my mother's grief-stricken face. I could not have borne the guilt. In general, I was not in need of dogmatic parenting, because I was an anxious sort of kid— which is neither good nor bad, just the way I was.

In the wake of a storm, consider what's going on with your child and the sort of child she is. If it's clear—from the look on *her* face or from her comments—that she feels guilty and awful about what happened, don't make her feel more awful. If you make her feel more awful, she'll just resent you for it. Avoid an inclination to induce guilt, promote shame, or hammer home a lesson.

A parent's urge is to lecture at a point when, say, an adolescent has had a run-in with a police officer or banged up the car. So Mom or Dad says, "Listen, kid, you got off lucky this time, but you have to be *really careful,* this is *really serious,* and if you *keep doing stuff like this* . . ." When you say, "See! What did I tell you?!" in all the ways you can think of, you're not really helping. These are all arguments that your teen has probably run through her own mind ten times already. Adolescents tell me, "I knew it was serious. I got arrested, of course it was serious. My parents didn't have to give me this lecture, they treat me like I'm stupid."

When a teen interfaces with the legal system, the police officer or the court worker usually aims to put a scare into her, to advise her what the circumstances are and orient her to how the system works. In most cases, that's sufficient. Most kids aren't interested in run-ins with the law. That doesn't mean you are lenient. You don't say, "Okay, forget about it." But if you know your child is already torturing herself about what happened, or has the basic right-and-wrong concepts down, then don't add to her burden. Try to use the event in a way that would be productive: "Okay, let's talk about what might be helpful in the future to avoid this kind of thing. What did you learn? Where did you go wrong here? Should you have not hung out with those kids?" That's a discussion that can be held around getting drunk or taking the car without permission or participating in trashing a friend's parents' house while they weren't home.

On the other hand, if your teen *doesn't* seem to feel somewhat guilty and awful, then it might be useful to stress the point that her behavior could have had extremely serious results. Again, however, you don't want to start out by saying, "You have simply got to be more careful or you're going to be in big trouble, and this isn't going to go unpunished, and your father is going to have something to say about all this . . ." That approach can easily prompt an unrepentant child to become defensive. And that's bad, because the minute she becomes defensive, she changes her story—even to herself *(It wasn't my fault, and the reason it wasn't my fault is because you think it was all my fault).* She is forced into revisionist history, and the last thing she can acknowledge is the truth. (The truth might be, *I was really scared, I was just walking along and the next thing I knew I was in a police car.)*

You're saying, "Let's talk about this." And if your child says, which she will 83 percent of the time, "I don't want to talk about it," it's appropriate to reply, "Okay, we don't have to do that now. Later, we will." Sometimes an adolescent thinks that by not discussing the incident, she defers whatever punishment awaits. Separate those two elements. Say, "I am deeply concerned about what happened. Until we talk about it and I find out what was going on, I think you ought to stay home in the evenings."

When a Child Needs Special Help

When a teen has gone through or is in the midst of a period of real trouble, perhaps in one of the ways I described in the previous chapter, two special requirements come into play: First, *he* needs an extra measure of structure, more so than is usually the case after run-of-the-mill acting up or breaking the ground rules; second, his *parents* need help and support if they're to be effective. They, too, can lose their compass pretty easily. So the following suggestions are critical.

Keep in touch with the other adults who've become involved with your teen.

Seek information from whoever is working with him—not for the purpose of ferreting out confidential material but to obtain parenting information.

If he's seeing a mental health practitioner, have a meeting with the therapist or program leader. This is a way to find both support and instruction, and it's especially important when a child has returned from a highly regimented residential treatment program. Ask what kinds of rules or actions on your part would be appropriate. Sometimes a parent says, "My child doesn't need curfews, we've never done that." The therapist may suggest, "You might want to impose curfews now, just to be sure he's not tempted to stay out late and run into some kids he's trying to stay away from for a while." You might hear that your child should have an occasional blood or urine test, if he's coming off substance abuse. You may learn that your teen would benefit from spending more time with you over the next month or two.

Keep in touch with the teacher or school counselor who became involved in your child's "case." Partly, this tells your teen there's an alliance trying to support her—and that's one less crack for her to fall through or one less split for her to exploit *(My teacher knows what Mom doesn't, Mom knows what my teacher doesn't)*.

Outline the specific steps you will be taking to help your child keep his promise.

If he's promised to quit smoking pot, quit dealing drugs, or get off alcohol, the environment isn't going to make that easy for him. You need to help. Let him know you'll be maintaining a greater vigilance concerning his whereabouts and his activities. This might include saying:

- "Sometimes, if I'm getting worried about what's going on, I may want to check out your room, and I'll ask you to go with me and reassure me that there's no problem."

- "I'd like you to phone me at work when you get out of school, just to check in."

- "I've told your teacher I'll be calling her once a week for a while, just to make sure I'm keeping up with what's going on in school."

- "I've asked the therapist to let me know if there's any difficulty about your making it to group on time."

- "I know you're not going to like this, but I'm going to ask you every evening if you remembered to take your medication."

All these rules and regulations can be presented in a matter-of-fact way, as something the child needs to do or needs to live with. Some rules and regulations are negotiable; these aren't. But tone—how you convey them—is the key to not coming across like a drill sergeant. You're showing that you intend to support him in what you realize is a difficult struggle. You will be the hovering parental presence made a little more visible, for as long as necessary.

Involve the family.

Don't assume that all the newly imposed structure must be absorbed by your adolescent. Often, the family needs to adopt some changes as well. To continue my analogy, you don't keep a dish of M&Ms out on the front hall table anymore if you learn your child is diabetic.

It's an excellent idea to discuss, family-meeting style, what might need adjustment, being careful not to blame the target child but to review the environment and the household in order to see what family members can do to be supportive. Here are some useful strategies.

Develop a more predictable rhythm to the day, or a new routine. If nobody's sat down to breakfast together in the past five years, this might be a good time to try to do so. Everyone gets up twenty minutes earlier, gathers in the kitchen, and runs down the upcoming events for the day, which might include that Becky is staying after school for band practice and Jeremy is going to group.

Invest in a mutual goal. Such as an exercise program. Say, "You know, we all ought to try to get in a little better shape. Who's game to start jogging with me?" Doing something that's tough but doing it together makes it easier for the teen who's working at reforming; it also keeps her from feeling as if she's being singled out as bad or wrong.

Eliminate obvious temptations. If alcohol has been your teen's problem, say, "We're going to remove all the liquor from the house, because we don't need it around and then it won't be a temptation to you." Do not overreact or point a finger, such as by implying, "Geez, now we can't even keep a few bottles of wine here because you can't handle it."

Close the family circle around your child a little more closely, if that seems wise. Deal wherever you can deal, wherever you see an opening. That might be to encourage your adolescent to get back in contact with a cousin who lives in another town, the kid he used to play with on long-ago summer vacations. Maybe persuade him to go to his uncle's fortieth birthday party next month. Say, "Uncle Harry's party isn't going to be a barrel of fun for you, but you're part of the family, and we'd like you to be there. If you're there just for half an hour, that would be fine."

All this is coming to some informed agreement that stretches your child, and sometimes you as well.

How to React to Your Teen's Reactions

Through the strategies I've outlined, you are saying to your adolescent, "We want you to make good decisions for yourself. That is our ultimate goal. Some of your recent secretive behaviors, as you know, were not the result of good decisions on your part. So we're setting some limits and imposing some consequences. We've told you what we expect, what you need to do in order to regain our trust and confidence, and how we will support you in these difficult efforts."

A lovely response from your teen would be, "Okay, Mom, okay, Dad, you're right. I was a jerk. I'm not going to do that stuff anymore, and I am going to try to redeem myself in your eyes by accepting these limits and consequences." It's not *impossible* that you'll receive such a reaction, but, be prepared to be met with one or another more likely response.

The defiant stance: "You can't make me."

This, of course, is true. Acknowledge as much. It's certainly not possible to prevent an adolescent from walking out the front door and breaking a grounding consequence. But perhaps this is an appropriate time to point out to him that a lot of what he takes for granted in his daily life—simple, unconsidered things such as watching TV, having a phone in his room—are in fact privileges that you have extended to him. Ideally, the defiant stance will not require that you go to this extreme, but you do have rights of ownership to everything a minor child possesses and you can remove those items if you want. He might need to hear, "No, we can't make you, but we're dedicated to helping you change your behavior for the better, and we might have to prove how serious we are by removing your TV or your computer or your phone."

The personal attack: "Who are you to talk?"

One of the tactics adolescents often use when they're cornered is to up the emotional ante by launching a personal attack: "That's pretty funny, you telling me not to smoke, you just quit two years ago, and you grew up in the sixties, I know you did pot." "Who are you to tell me I can't spend time with my boyfriend, you had me when you were nineteen and you weren't even married to Dad yet." A teen with a little intellectual prowess or a little history of your life can say hurtful things.

Try to step back from it. Don't go toe-to-toe and refute your child's argument. Actually, try to ignore the words during these kinds of altercations, because you are dealing with a trapped animal. It's a primitive flight-or-fight response. Parents often treat these as rational arguments they must counter, but they're not; the adolescent is simply picking up anything available and throwing it in an effort to retaliate. Sometimes children during this stage say things they don't mean and sometimes they say things expressly because of the impact they know they'll have.

The denial: "I didn't do anything."

Most teenagers usually prefer to tell the truth, until that stops working in their favor; then they start lying. If your child, let's say, has been caught smoking pot once, he'll own up to the fact. If it's repeated behavior, he's unlikely to say, "Yeah, you're right, that was the sixth time I was out smoking dope with my friends." He's more likely to deny any such thing ever happened.

If you *do* get the truth, reward that: "I'm very glad you told me. I don't condone that behavior, I wish you hadn't done it, it was wrong, but I appreciate that you were honest with me." When you're pretty certain you're not hearing the truth, when lying is getting out of hand, you need to confront the matter. This is when you might say, "You have to know that because of what's been happening recently, I assume or suspect that you're lying to us a lot. So as part of the new rules we're establishing, I'm going to ask you questions when I think you're not telling the truth and you're going to have to tell me why I'm wrong. If you say you'll be at Billy's house to do some studying and I think you're lying, you will have to tell me I'm wrong in a way that will keep me from calling up Billy's folks."

In this way, you put the responsibility for what follows on your teen rather than on you. And dealing with the facts honestly must be part of his way back to your trust and confidence.

The debate: "I don't agree."

I spoke earlier about the teen's typical confusion of agreement and understanding, as when she says, "But you don't *understand*, Mom, all the movies let out at eleven-fifteen, so there's no way you can give me an eleven o'clock curfew." To which, I advised you to reply, "I do understand when the movies let out, but I cannot agree to extend the eleven o'clock curfew this time." This is somewhat the same situation. Ideally, you want your teen both to understand the reason for and to agree with the limits and consequences you are setting.

However, if she doesn't agree *and* there is no room for further negotiation, at least make sure she understands: "Okay, I just took the car away for two weeks, and maybe you don't understand why. Well, here's why . . ."

When your adolescent rebels against the consequences and limits you have set, he's likely to pull out the emotional stops in one or another of these ways. As a parent, the trick is not to become caught and not to retaliate. Easier said than done. It's difficult *not* to be engaged emotionally in escalating circumstances and to say, "Okay, let's just calm down." And sometimes you do need to vent; that's preferable, actually, to cutting the child off emotionally, or reacting to his fury with a kind of chilly neutrality. Your expression of anger, which of course must not involve physical abuse of any sort, is, after all, a sign of connection; the size of the upset reflects the size of the commitment. A teenager really can grasp it—that if you didn't love him so much you wouldn't bother being mad at him. (Or, if you think he's not grasping it, you can tell him.)

But your child should be able to express anger to you without being crushed like a bug. Adolescents complain all the time, "It's okay for my dad to chew me out, but if I say, 'Hey Dad, you're no paragon of virtue yourself,' I get, 'You shut your damn mouth!' " A teen's expression of anger is okay, and then she needs some guidelines for how to do that more acceptably. After her outburst, you might say, "I understand you're angry. It is not okay, however, to punch the wall and it's not okay to call me names. So let's talk about what's making you mad, and I'll tell you what I was responding to. We'll go over this all again if that would be helpful."

In general, try not to get into tit for tat, which of course is what we tell our kids all the time ("Just because your little brother hit you doesn't mean you should hit him back. You're older and stronger than he is"). It's up to you de-escalate these situations and to see at a process level what's going on, beyond the words that are spoken or the emotions that are charging the atmosphere.

Here's the final point I'd make about repairing the trust between you and your wayward adolescent: Prepare to spend time on all this.

At the beginning of the chapter, I mentioned how easy it is for parents to dodge the whole issue of imposing rules and consequences, to talk themselves out of it—partly because getting into it with a teenager sounds as if it's going to take a lot of time and effort and energy. Yes, unfortunately, it will. A child changing for the better doesn't work just on the honor system, even though you'd like it to.

In general, parents report that the restrictions on their own adult lives are among the most stressful aspects of being mothers and fathers. We don't like it that we can't have as many parties as we'd enjoy, we can't be gone from the house as often as we'd wish. One consequence is that we promote our children to adulthood before they're ready, because it's a nuisance to devote the extra time they need as children. That's especially true, and maybe especially stressful, when an adolescent is going through a period of needing more structure, more paying attention to. But this must be your priority, for as long as it takes. This is about rapprochement, restoring harmony and friendly relations, and pointing your child down the better path. Especially with an adolescent, that takes time. Whatever difficulty your child is dealing with isn't your fault necessarily, but it is your responsibility.

I ask teens, "What do you hate most that your parents say to you, what really hurts?" Invariably, they tell me, "It's when they say, 'I'm so disappointed in you.' Or 'I just can't trust you again.' " Even though your child may balk and protest and go on the attack, or just tell you to your face, "Leave me alone," he really at some level does want you to engage with him in the ways I've outlined in this chapter, even though it's not much fun for anyone. He does know they're right. He does want you to see him as worthwhile, as worthy of your trust. In fact, it's a fine idea to articulate this in so many words, to say, "I don't want to lay down these rules and limits and consequences, but I'm going to do it because it needs to be done and because you're worth it."

CHAPTER 8

Other Kids' Secrets

*When Your Teen Becomes Involved in a
Friend's Private Problems*

Ellie, thirteen, was good friends with Susan. One day at the tail end of eighth grade, Susan confided a troubling secret: Susan's divorced mother had remarried, and now the household consisted of Susan, her mom, her new stepfather, Joe, and Joe's thirteen-year-old son from a previous marriage, Derek. On three occasions over the past two months, Derek had come into Susan's room in the middle of the night and attempted to fondle her. Susan asked her mother if they could install a lock on her bedroom door, and her mom said they might be moving next year so she didn't want to bother with a lot of changes now. Feeling embarrassed, she hinted at what was happening, but her mom didn't seem to be listening and brushed her off. "She's so into this new marriage," Susan told Ellie, "she doesn't want anything to go wrong."

Deeply upset for her friend, Ellie said maybe she should talk to one of their teachers, or call the police. Or she, Ellie, would make the call for her. "No, don't say anything," Susan shouted. "If Derek gets reported, it'll ruin everything, and my stepfather will kill me." That evening, Ellie's instinct was to ask her parents for advice. But she didn't, fearing that her mother or father would dash right in and insist on phoning Susan's mom immediately, and Susan would be in for it at home. She didn't know if Susan was right—would they literally kill her? If Ellie did call the police herself, she thought, what would she say? Anyway, how could she know about the whole thing if Susan hadn't told her, so wouldn't Susan still get in trouble?

Four days later, early on Saturday morning, Susan packed up a few clothes and took a bus to her aunt's apartment in another city, which turned out to be a smart action in the long run. The aunt treated Susan's situation seriously and was instrumental in bringing about changes: She talked candidly to Susan's mother, and it was arranged that Susan would spend the summer with her aunt. When Susan returned home to start tenth grade, Derek had already left for a boarding school in which his father had enrolled him. Susan, her mom, and her stepfather began some family counseling.

Ellie had confused emotions about it all. When Susan "ran away," she was horrified. Over the summer, the two girls had no contact except for one phone call, which, Ellie said, "left her feeling really guilty, because she sounded so uptight—she didn't especially want to be living with her aunt." Three months later, when Susan returned, Ellie was glad that things seemed to be going better for her, but she felt she'd let her friend down in some important way.

This young teen's involvement in her friend's bad scene points to one highly charged aspect of adolescent life. Sometimes a child is confided in by another child and warned not to tell a soul. Sometimes a child is confided in and seems to be asked for help out of a jam. And sometimes, nobody's talking, but a child unwittingly and maybe unwillingly is aware of a friend's behaviors that are dangerous. Whatever the situation, the teen who becomes privy to a friend's worrisome secret almost always finds herself between a rock and a hard place.

She may feel responsible, as if it's up to her to be a savior and to make the right decisions, or up to her to protect her friend from getting into trouble.

She doesn't know if or how she should bring others into the picture. An adolescent sometimes consults with other friends, but together they come up with no bright plans, or they reach a consensus that they don't have enough information to go on, or everybody has a different idea.

She doesn't know what to expect from any adults she might tell. Parents can overreact; "official" people such as teachers or police are an unknown quantity, and turning to one of them, she thinks, might mean setting off a nasty chain of events.

And if the friend has sworn her to secrecy, the thought of violating that trust is abhorrent. Fierce loyalty toward peers, and fears that "telling" will destroy the precious friendship, can outweigh her sense that everybody could use some outside help right now.

That adds up to a lot of stress. Interestingly, but maybe not surprisingly, popular teenagers are often the recipients of others' secrets. You may know that your child—because of her admirable character traits of empathy and caring—is a confidante to many of her friends; she's the one others go to with their problems. But life can be difficult for the helpful child, because she's thrust into the middle of various dilemmas without much guidance on how to handle them. One girl told her mother, "This is weird. I'm doing great, but all this horrible stuff is going on with kids I know. It really upsets me." She was carrying around the heavy burdens of friends.

A parent sometimes can take an active role in helping a child's friend; under certain circumstances, Mom or Dad *must* step in. But a parent can *always* be a sounding board, make suggestions, come up with practical information, and offer emotional support when a son or daughter has been let in on a

friend's troubling secret. In this chapter, I look at some ideas
on how to fill those roles.

Preparing Your Child to
Handle the Secrets of Friends

To begin, talk to her generally about the rules of confiding.

Thinking ahead, as a good parent does, you probably had
the you're-growing-up-now talk—or more than one—with
your preteen. Maybe that included suggesting to your very
attractive, precocious daughter that she would be receiving a
lot of attention from boys in the years ahead, she might not
always feel comfortable about it, and you'd be happy to discuss
with her any situations she found tricky. Maybe you talked to
your son about the changing social scene that he'd be entering
and how he'd probably be going to parties where there was
drinking or kids were smoking pot. All those parental messages were acknowledgments that your child was moving into
a more independent and more complicated stage of existence;
the world was going to look a little different, and it wouldn't
always be clear how to act.

Have a "secrets" talk with your child as well—a discussion
about difficult emotional/friendship issues that may arise. And
again, when she's ten or eleven—before she's in the thick of adolescent social life—is an excellent time to do so. Here are the
four main ideas to get across and how you might express them.

Bad stuff happens to good kids. You don't want to start
such a conversation on a note of doom, by running down a list
of pitfalls and dangers that lie ahead. You can, however, say
something like, "I know your friends are very important to
you, and they're going to keep on being very important. You'll

probably start spending more time with them and less with us. Some kids you'll meet in middle school or high school—maybe some kids you know now—might run into problems of one sort or another. And maybe they'll talk to you about their problems and say nobody else can know anything about what's going on. They'll ask you to keep it secret, because that's what it means to be a friend."

Some secrets are not okay to keep. When your child does run into a secrets situation, she'll have to make several judgment calls on her own: Is this information she can keep to herself, or is it information grown-ups really should know about? Now, beforehand, give her some guidelines on how to go about that:

"Let's imagine some secrets you could hear. Your best friend says, 'Mom thinks I'm studying in the library after school, but I'm really going to the mall. Don't tell anybody.' You might have some ideas about that, you might think she shouldn't be lying to her mom, but probably you wouldn't feel you had to pass on the news. In fact, if you did, it might feel like tattling. Sometimes, though, it's not fair for a friend to make you promise not to tell anybody. So you might have to figure out some things to know what to do.

"You might have to ask yourself, 'Am I frightened by my friend's behavior, or really worried about her?' 'Do I think she's going to hurt herself or somebody else?' 'Am I afraid that she might die?' 'Is there a chance that she's not telling me everything and the situation is actually worse than she said?' This isn't easy. You would feel terrible for your friend, and it might be very hard to break your promise and talk to somebody else. If you tell, maybe your friend will never talk to you again. And that will hurt. But what if you don't tell, and your friend gets pregnant, or ODs on drugs, or tries to kill herself?

That will hurt more. Some secrets are not okay to keep, and it really is right to tell an adult if you're worried or frightened by something your friend has told you."

Parents can be helpful. Your message is: "It's okay to put me in the loop. Come and talk to me. I won't do anything rash, I won't do anything without discussing it with you, but we can put our heads together and see what ideas we come up with."

Other adults can be helpful too. Acknowledge that although it's been you all along as the fount of wisdom and support regarding friendship matters, you realize that's not necessarily going to stay the same over these years. You're letting your child know that you accept the shift into Stage 2 parenting (obviously, you're not saying so in just those words), and there will be times she may *not* want to put you in the loop. And that's all right, as long as she has other reliable resources to turn to.

Say, "If you're really worried about something going on with a friend, you need to tell someone who'll be helpful. That doesn't have to be me. You might not feel right about coming to me, and that's okay, I don't need to know everything. So, suppose you found out your friend had a problem or was doing something scary, who do you think you might tell, who would you feel comfortable talking to?" Maybe an older brother, a religious leader, or a caring neighbor will come to her mind; you can mention that though she doesn't yet know all the teachers she'll be having, there will surely be one or two she will come to like and feel all right about confiding in.

In this kind of "secrets" talk, you're getting across an added, unspoken message as well, which is all to the good: "This is what to think about and these are actions to take if you ever find yourself in the middle of your *own* tough or scary issues."

Problem Solving Together with Your Teen

When your child does come to you about a friend's secret problem or behavior, what do you do next? Throughout any developments that follow, try to maintain an atmosphere that says this isn't a matter of you, a parent, versus your child and her best friend, but of you and your child thinking out loud and acting jointly because of a realistic fear that something bad could happen. The following questions you might ask your teen will convey that message and will move along a problem-solving talk.

"How are you feeling about this secret your friend told you?"

Your fifteen-year-old lets on that her best friend's boyfriend is planning to steal a car and the two of them are going to drive to Nevada and get married. This, obviously, is unsettling news, and your child is probably agitated herself, along with, perhaps, experiencing a little thrill about the whole thing. Get her feet on the ground: "Oh, gosh, that sounds a bad idea to me. How do you feel about that?" This rather shrinklike question is useful because it encourages her to explore her emotions and because it gives both of you a moment to pause for a breath. Maybe she says, "I'm really, really worried." Say, "I can imagine you are. You probably don't know what to do. I don't know what to do either, right now, let's talk about it."

Sometimes you need to calm your child down, in order to help her calm her friend down or to be able to think clearly about a possible plan.

"What do you know exactly about your friend's situation?"

Getting as many details as possible is often critical. For example, adolescents sometimes confide in a friend about a difficult scene at home, and these are tricky situations that are occurring at some remove from you both.

One girl told her mother, "Sara's being abused by her father, and I don't know what to do. Could you do something about it?" Her mother asked, "What has she told you, what happens? Is she hurt? Is her mom aware of this?" The daughter answered, "I don't know. She says he's really mean and she hates him." A boy told his father one evening that he was upset about his friend Sean, because Sean's father was always drinking. Sometimes Sean didn't go to school, because his dad got drunk the night before and he was afraid his dad would start pushing around his mom in the morning, so Sean stayed home to protect her.

When information is coming to you secondhand and the details are sketchy, there's always a possibility that it's a story the friend made up or embroidered on to get your child's attention. Even when you and your teen are convinced the story is legitimate, it's hard to know what would be an appropriate action. In either case, it's probably most helpful to suggest that your child might be able to mention the situation to an adult who knows the friend and maybe the friend's parents, and is in a position to intervene in an official capacity. For example, "We don't know exactly what it's like in Sara's home, but here's something you can do. If Sara doesn't want to tell anybody else, you can go to your school counselor and talk to her. She's trained to handle family situations like this."

If a friend has made a threat to hurt himself, encourage

your child to think about whether the threat is serious. Your teen says, "Matt has been acting really weird lately, and today he told me he wants to kill himself and I'm worried." You might then ask, "What else did he say? Do you believe him? Is that something he really might do, in your opinion?" Your child replies, "Yeah, I do believe him, because he showed me this bunch of pills he took from his mom's medicine cabinet, he had them in his backpack, and he's got it figured out how he's going to take the train out to the beach next Friday night and take all these pills and die." That sounds like a serious plan, not just melodramatic talk, and your child—or your child and you—must act on it.

"What have you thought about doing, and what have you tried so far?"

Ask your child what thoughts she's had, or what she thinks is possible. We sometimes don't consider teens as intelligent sources with the ability to analyze a situation objectively and usefully, but often they are surprisingly skilled at problem solving. By the time a child has taken the bold step of confiding in an adult, she may already have run various solutions through her own mind. And she knows her friend better than you do and has an idea what will work and what won't.

Those may include getting the friend some practical help, or persuading her to put off a risky plan for another couple of weeks until she's had more time to think about it, or suggesting they go together to talk to the school psychologist. She may have thought about taking her friend to a crisis center. Or maybe she's already been trying to bolster her friend's confidence so that she feels better about herself in general.

"Can you urge your friend to talk to her parents or to another adult?"

This is almost always the first line of approach, encouraging the child with the problem to take the risk of confiding in her parents or someone else close to her. Often, though, the adolescent who's carrying around a friend's secret says, "Yeah, sure, I told her she's got to tell her mom, but she says her mom will just freak out and tell her dad, and then her dad will hit the ceiling."

So part of this discussion might include asking your teen if she herself would feel comfortable calling her friend's parents and bringing them in on the secret. Sometimes, that's actually what a troubled child hopes will happen. You might say, "I understand that Lucy said not to tell anybody, but maybe she really wants her mom to know what's going on and she just can't talk about it herself."

A surprisingly large number of adolescents feel they can't tell their parents about a dilemma they're having, and so they essentially empower a friend to do it for them. The child in trouble is hoping to be "discovered" and to have her parents come to her aid, but she's unable or unwilling to admit what's happening. The issue may be depression, pregnancy, cutting, social predicaments such as a girl feeling that a boy is taking advantage of her and doesn't know how to stop it. That adolescent may not necessarily *ask* her friend, in so many words, to call her mom or dad, but by making her own worry so palpable or her risky behaviors so over the top, she pushes the friend to take action. This is when the confided-in child calls and says, "I thought I should talk to you, Mrs. Johnson, because I'm worried about Janice. It seems like a lot of guys are hitting on her and she looks really unhappy."

This is a brave act. Ideally, Janice's mom will take that

information to heart and listen carefully, because the friend has violated a major adolescent norm by crossing into parent territory.

"Could we pass on some helpful information to your friend?"

Often, you can feed useful suggestions to the affected child through your child. If the friend is insisting nobody can know, she may feel okay about talking to a third party with no emotional stake in the situation. So you might say to your teen, "If Katie's upset, I know a really kind social worker who might help. I bet she'd be happy to talk to Katie. Why don't you give her the number?"

Or "There's a Planned Parenthood office in town. You could look up that number and make sure your friend has it. That's a good place for her to get some counseling and find out what her options are."

Or "You know, there's something called the Alateen Information Center. Maybe Sean could check that out."

"Do you want me to talk to your friend's parents?"

Your child may want to contact the friend's parents herself. But offer to help. If she says, "I'm thinking of calling her mom, but I feel kind of nervous," say, "I think that's a good idea, but I see how it would be hard. Let's get together on this. Would you like me to call her parents? Or we can drive over to her house right away. Do you think that's the right thing to do?" You do not want to suggest, "Well, your best friend might be suicidal, you better make that call because you gotta grow up and do things that are hard." At times, parents must act for their adolescents.

If the friend's secret involves killing himself or another person, if it involves buying a gun, if you and your child are convinced there's clear and imminent danger, you *must* act to protect someone's life. Even if it turns out you're wrong, you do not have the luxury to wait it out and consider various approaches. You may need to say to your own child, "This is a secret it's not okay to keep. Yes, her parents are going to be upset, and yes, maybe she'll feel you betrayed her. But the alternative is that you might be visiting her in jail, or she might really hurt herself. I know you want to honor your friend's trust and your promise, but you have to take your own concerns seriously too. Keeping everybody safe is the most important thing right now, and the rest you can work out later."

In many less immediately dangerous situations, however, if or when a parent should intervene and contact the other parents is a judgment call. Here's a common scenario: Rachel tells her mother that Polly, Rachel's best friend, is pregnant and she has sworn Rachel to secrecy. And the two sets of parents have known each other for years. Of course, Rachel's mom thinks, *Those people are my friends. I've got to tell them. If Rachel was pregnant, I for sure would want to know, and if I found out some other mother knew and didn't tell me, I'd be really angry and hurt.* The child's friend's secret becomes a personally prickly issue for the child's parent.

There are no hard-and-fast rules. But in the case of a pregnant friend, if the pregnancy is early enough and the girl isn't planning to run off with her boyfriend or attempt a self-induced abortion, there's time to consider a few approaches and see what happens. The goal, always, is to persuade the girl to talk to her parents herself, so they can problem-solve together. If Polly's relationship with her mom is such that she feels she absolutely can't confide in her, another responsible adult—a teacher, a trained listener, an individual in a crisis center or hotline—might give her the support she needs to take that difficult step.

Parent-to-parent phone calls or in-person discussions are tough. In some cases, deciding if a troubled child is a danger to himself or other people is difficult. And whatever the dilemma, talking to another father or mother about his or her own adolescent requires great finesse. You learn from your teen that his best friend is dealing pot or her friend is having sex with six boys. Conveying your child's and your concern can so easily come out sounding like, "Your son is doing criminal stuff, and how come you haven't noticed?" or "Your daughter needs therapy, quick, and where have you been?" It might be useful to say, "I have been talking with my son. He's concerned about some things that are going on, some things involving your child. I thought you might like to hear what I have heard."

These are personal and hard decisions to make. Many times, the most genuinely useful path is to help your child help his friend find help—and then continue to follow up with your own teen and ask how the solutions the two of you explored are working. Again, it's tempting to think, *Okay, I guess that turned out all right, and I'm real glad it's over with.* But a friend's difficult secret is something you've taken on together, you and your teen; don't withdraw your support too soon.

All these are highly meaningful conversations to have with a young adolescent. You're laying out responsibilities she may face or does face, and helping her develop adult skills: weighing information, using her common sense and trusting her instincts, risking the anger of a friend for the sake of the friend's well-being, and reaching out for advice and help when that's uncomfortable to do. Along the way, she learns more about her values and her strengths.

CHAPTER 9

Parenting Partnerships

*Working Together with Your Spouse and
the Other Adults in Your Teenager's World*

Adolescence can be overwhelming for the children living through it. That's why it's overwhelming for their parents too. We tend to hold fast to a nuclear notion, that Mom or Dad should be able to handle whatever bumps in the road appear. And if Mom or Dad can't handle them, something's going wrong. But as I have been suggesting throughout this book, we all need a little help from our friends (or from friendly strangers).

There's real wisdom to the notion that it takes a village to raise a child—not only in the sense that it's good to have other people keeping an eye out for your son or daughter. Stage 2 parenting really must be something of a community endeavor, because even good parents need a great deal of support. In this chapter, I explore some ideas on forming and cementing parenting partnerships—with other mothers and fathers who are tangling with many of the same issues; with other sensible adults for your child to know and talk to and, especially, with your teen's other parent.

What Married Parents Should Know

One of the most stressful aspects of raising adolescents is that when trouble is afoot, Mom and Dad are forced to deal not only with their child but also with their partnership. If you think your son is secretly shoplifting, now you're going to have to talk to your spouse about it. And is he or she going to see the situation the way you do? When two parents are on different wavelengths, it's all too easy to defeat each other and miss the boat in terms of what the child actually requires. So the following strategies are intended to suggest how to coordinate wavelengths.

Supply each other with regular updates on current events.

Your child might confide in you about some personal issue on her mind, and the confidence leads to a heartfelt mother-and-daughter talk. If you then share the whole saga with your spouse, and if Dad the next day says to his daughter, "Hi, honey, I heard you and Mom had a great talk last night," daughter is outraged. "You know, Mom, that was private, that's the last time I tell you anything," she says. Of course, as two adults who married each other and had kids, you might see nothing wrong with discussing a particular confidence with your spouse, prefacing it with, "Okay, you didn't hear this from me, but . . ." We do and can have secrets from our children, and that might be one of them.

But teens should know that you and your partner do talk together about the events in their lives—not necessarily intimate concerns that an adolescent would be mortified to have revealed to his or her opposite gender parent, but matters that are appropriate for everybody to be in on. They actually expect that to be the case and can be surprised or wounded when one or another parent doesn't seem to know what's going on. Occasionally I'd ask my daughter or son, "Hey, what's new? You still thinking about having that party?" and I'd hear, "Well, gee, Dad, don't you and Mom ever talk to each other? I just told her all about that yesterday."

At least give the illusion that you and your partner are both on the same page, and you do regularly keep each other informed about your children's lives.

Discuss limits and consequences.

If Mom says, "Okay, that's it, you're grounded for a week," and Dad comes home and says, "How come you're not out tonight?" your child will likely be disgusted over the lack of parental consistency. What's more, he's encouraged to exploit it: "I'll go to Mom because she'll never talk to Dad, then later on I can talk to Dad and tell him Mom says it's okay." Your fifteen-year-old is just as good at this kind of manipulation as the five-year-old who learns in a hurry that Mom gets in a swivet about somebody eating a cookie before dinner but Dad doesn't.

When a child is acting up or acting out, it's especially critical that two parents know about and agree on any consequences that may be set. It's not always easy. Many parents must be gone from home a lot of the time—airline pilots or individuals working night shifts. That creates a complication, when Mom says, "Wait until your father gets home in three weeks, you're going to be in real hot water." But parenting can't be entirely spontaneous. Some advance planning and coordination about limits and consequences is essential.

Acknowledge which one of you is better at what.

Old gender stereotypes do still pertain, although less so than in previous generations—parents, probably especially fathers, saying, "Boys will be boys, so he had a little beer, what's the big deal?" A father will approve of an adolescent son having sex (which might lay to rest the issue of whether or not the boy is gay) but is appalled about a sexually active daughter. Both parents may tend to overreact with girls while being more permissive than is wise with the boys.

Gender differences sometimes are and sometimes aren't relevant. I often tell parents, "You're up against it. Don't be afraid to use any edge you have."

For example, it's often useful for a father to talk to his son or a mother to talk to her daughter, because each adult has had at least some points of similarity with the child in the course of growing up. Sometimes your lack of understanding because you're of a different gender makes you more likely either to give in or to be rigid, when sharing information and offering suggestions to a teen is what's called for. I remember talking to my daughter at times about some issue concerning dating, curfews, or fashion, and being persuaded by her that my concern was silly ("Oh, come on Dad, it's not a problem, everybody does this . . ."). Then when mentioning the discussion to my wife, I'd hear, "Oh, geez, she pulled that one on you? I used to do that to my dad all the time. You're such a patsy." She, being a grown-up girl like her daughter would become, had the experience to say to our teen, "I used to sneak out wearing things like that too, and here's why I learned it wasn't such a great idea . . ."

In addition, much depends on you, your spouse, and your child. You may have a couple of children, and one parent simply seems to do a better job with one of the kids, irrespective of gender. What works best is a function of the kind of rapport and relationship you have. Or you adopt different approaches to different matters. This usually comes up around who's going to talk to the kids about sex. At first blush, we'd tend to say, dads will most comfortably have that kind of heart-to-heart session with sons (not that such talks are ever actually comfortable). In fact, an adolescent boy who gets along well with his mother might have a truly useful exchange with her about some of the emotional issues that come along with sexual activity—issues his father may ignore.

Again, the hallmark of good parenting is strategizing together. That might mean saying to your spouse, "Okay, Sally is into some bad behavior, Rick is doing some things we don't want him to do. How should we approach this? One, we need to know how to back each other up, and two, we can use the insights each of us has about our kids so we can develop a way to help. You deal with her about this, I'll deal with him about that." Play to your own individual parenting strengths.

Try to see eye-to-eye about your teen's activities.

In some households, Mom and Dad are perpetually on different sides of the fence regarding the worrisome quotient of their child's secretive behaviors. One is bothered; the other doesn't see what all the fuss is about. A fifteen-year-old girl described this scene in her family: "I've been bummed out about stuff this year. Boyfriend stuff and other things, and I know I'm in a down mood at home a lot of the time, like when we're having dinner. Then my mom starts getting all bummed out herself and asking me if everything's okay, is something bothering me. So I just want to get away from them and not feel I'm being forced into talking. Then they start arguing with each other. I'm upstairs in my room, and I hear my dad saying, 'Just get off her back, leave her alone,' and my mom's saying, 'Why don't you try to be a little more sensitive and observant once in a while?' Then I think I'm ruining everything for everybody."

For some teens, like this girl, these kinds of parental disagreements induce guilt or added gloominess. Others exploit such differences. Seventeen-year-old Will, who'd been getting in a lot of trouble with marijuana smoking and dealing, said he knew he was causing a rift between his parents, who were always attempting to come to some agreement about what he needed. He *wanted* the rift, he said, "because I figured I'd just wear them down sooner or later, and they'd decide to leave me alone."

It really is a necessary effort to try to get on the same page with your partner regarding your adolescent's worrisome behavior—without that effort taking the form of bickering or personal attacks. If his insistence on privacy or his noncommunication is starting to get you really worried, and your spouse brushes it off, show him some neutral material to bolster your argument. Suggest he read this book. Talk to a trained listener who has some knowledge of adolescents.

The effort can be especially critical if a child might benefit from professional help. Often in therapy, when two parents come to talk about their child, the father says, "Well, his mother seems to be very worried about this, but I don't really see it as a big problem myself," or "Apparently his mom thinks he's really out of control." Fathers in general tend to be more resistant to the idea of outside help; it feels personally humiliating, embarrassing, or annoying to Dad that he's been cornered into finding therapy for his son or daughter. That father then often doesn't want to get with the program, and the message can easily sabotage the child's improvement. This is when a father might say, "Oh, you're going to that shrink again today. Didn't you just see him last week?" or "You're having another meeting with that person your mom likes?"

All these suggestions apply as well when two parents aren't getting along too swimmingly, or are, in fact, divorced or divorcing—but here some additional strategies are necessary. Research shows that individuals in bad partnerships experience parenting as more stressful. That's particularly true during adolescence, because, first, children during these ages have the talent and wit to capitalize on parental stress more effectively, and, second, they're capable of more dangerous behaviors than they were when they were younger. Dealing drugs or sexual acting out are worse than stomping on toys or writing with crayons on the wall.

What Divorced or Single Parents Should Know

Kevin, fourteen, was caught between warring parents who were in the process of divorcing. The split was a hostile one, with the two seldom speaking to each other and financial matters a sticking point. When Kevin returned from a weekend with his dad, his mom fished for information. Any small bit of news—such as that Kevin and his father went shopping in a home furnishings store Saturday afternoon and Dad bought a twelve-bottle wine rack—prompted a grilling: "Is he entertaining people? You know, having dinner parties? So he's all of a sudden into fancy wine now?" From his father, Kevin often heard, "You go home and tell your mother that she'd better stop snooping around."

Over the course of the year and a half that his parents' marriage was coming undone, Kevin discovered that it was safest for him to say nothing much at all. He essentially shut down, telling his parents little about what was going on in his own life as well. Wise beyond his years, Kevin plowed his energy and focus into maintaining himself on an even course and keeping up his school grades, and spent as much time as possible with one friend or hanging out with his kid sister. He did what he needed to survive, through a tiring and lonely struggle.

Peter, fifteen, split his time between his mother and father, each of whom seemed to be trying to win the title of favorite parent. He lived with his mother during the week and spent most weekends and school holidays with his father. Typically, by Thursday or Friday night he was really pushing the bounds of acceptable behavior, doing sneaky stuff and making his mom increasingly nervous. But Peter was something of a silver-tongued devil and could make a persuasive case to his mother about why it was all right for him to get home past his curfew or go to a downtown club. Besides, he knew she would be reluctant to get on his case and make a scene right before he was to leave and spend the next couple of days with his father. Peter actually articulated this quite clearly: "She wants my dad to think everything's going great at home because she and I have this great relationship and she's such a terrific parent. Then my dad is real easygoing on the weekends, and I don't get hit with a lot of rules and stuff. Basically, I sort of get them both where I want them."

Maggie, sixteen, lived with her mother, her eleven-year-old sister Lauren, and her stepfather of half a year. Since the stepfather had entered the scene, Maggie and Lauren had taken on different personae. Neither girl was happy about their new stepdad, but Lauren was unusually sweet and compliant, the good girl; Maggie, it seemed, had decided to be the bad girl and started having sex with several boys. Not just any boys. She went to some lengths to get together with the ones most likely to drive her mother to distraction. Maggie had shown up on two occasions with two different boys she was dating. Both were three years older than she, and both were school dropouts with no jobs and no plans.

Her mother didn't know if Maggie was sexually involved with them. When she asked once, Maggie's reply was, "Maybe. Why?" Her mom didn't ask again. All the parents involved with this adolescent were deeply concerned, and no one saw a way to rein her in. Maggie's father had also remarried, but he and his new wife had no greater success talking to her about her behavior. Stepfather Max was completely ignored by Maggie, so he concentrated on winning over young Lauren. Everybody was stumped.

The behaviors of these three teens show how two divorcing or divorced parents can foment unhappy or dangerous secrecy in a child. During the early stages of divorce and often for some time afterward, one or both parents can find it hard to keep up with what's going on with the kids. Mom or Dad or both experience what psychologist Judith Wallerstein termed "the diminished capacity to parent." They're distracted by their own anger or disequilibrium, by the need to deal with myriad unpleasant details, by real worries about money or houses or the future, and by the emotional needs of pursuing personal lives that are sometimes frightening or disturbing to their children. When new love partners enter the picture, interactions all around take a quantum leap in complexity. This is another of those times when parents can bail on their adolescents, and thus when adolescents—coping with their own upset and a loss of structure—can drift off into private lives that aren't good for them.

All that suggests several strategies critical for parents who are raising one adolescent from two separate places.

Remember that you're the adult.

I sometimes meet with squabbling parents to whom I would like to say, "Grow up, you two! Act like adults! You still have a shared parenting obligation, no matter how much you despise each other."

A shared parenting obligation means putting an adolescent's well-being first—and that includes not making him or her bear the brunt of your personal hostilities. We regularly admonish our children in one way or another, "Just because you're mad at somebody, it's not okay to let your anger get the better of you and make you do something dumb or hurtful." And yet parents all the time, in front of their children, launch verbal attacks or character assaults at each other. Sometimes, children pick up immature behaviors from their parents; just as often, however, a child living between fractious adults becomes a little smarter or a little more mature than they are. The teen might be able to say, "Well, Mom is having one of her fits again. It's just about Dad, that's the way they get."

But the child can pay a high price for maintaining that level of distance. Children of all ages are upset when parents do battle with each other, and a teen may be in danger of displaying some of the troubling behaviors I described in earlier chapters—internalizing or externalizing depression, anxiety, symptoms of deep loneliness. Sometimes, too, a teen is left essentially to parent himself in certain ways, a job for which he's not equipped.

Putting an adolescent's well-being first also means resisting any urge to turn him into a go-between. If teens dislike being interrogated about the details of their own lives, they *really* dislike being used as conveyors of information about the currently absent parent, as Kevin was, or being made the messenger concerning plans and schedules for two adults who can't stand talking to each other.

Maintain communication.

For the sake of your child, who is vulnerable now, you and your former spouse must talk. You must keep each other posted about how he's acting, about what kinds of structure each of you is providing, and about any consequences that need to be established.

Bad behavior in one home should lead to canceled privileges in the other home. Teens such as Peter, who played off one parent against the other, become extremely adept at working on their *parents'* vulnerabilities, sore points, and wishes to be liked. Peter would do a lot better in life—although it won't feel so to him—if his mother explained to his father about broken curfews and lying behavior with her, and if his father in turn saw to it that Peter didn't get to enjoy himself too much over the next weekend they shared.

Try to be flexible about arrangements.

For the amicably divorced parents of two daughters, life had been proceeding smoothly until the older child hit age thirteen. Before then, for the four years the parents had been apart, the girls lived with their mother and spent many school holidays and part of summer vacations with their father, who enjoyed taking them camping. That year, the camping expedition was still a treat for the nine-year-old, while the teen insisted she wouldn't go—she desperately wanted to remain with her friends. When both parents continued to lean heavily on maintaining the plan, she disappeared the night before the father was coming to collect the girls. After giving her parents a couple of hours of panic, she called from a friend's house, saying she wanted to stay there through the vacation period. Her parents finally gave up on the camping idea.

During a time when children become so intensely attached to their friends, and when those friendships are crucial to their very sense of existence, it's extremely wise for separated parents to revisit the old arrangements about visitations, joint custody, and so on. They may need to be recast, in order to accommodate a teen's increasing independence and shifting ideas about who should be making decisions for her.

Acknowledge the difficulty of the "interloper" parent.

Blended parent relationships—when there's a new stepparent in the family—more often than not are tremendously hard for children, at least at first and maybe for some time. The "new" parent, according to the child, has no rights at all.

In a common pattern, Mom and Dad divorce; Mom lives with the kids by herself for a while and does a fabulous job of bonding with them and helping them cope with the changed circumstances of their lives. Eventually, she falls in love and remarries. And suddenly, the children are without the full attention of their mother, and they're furious. The best way for them to deal with their anger is to attack the interloper. Stepparents in such situations are often kind, well-meaning, conciliatory individuals—who are ripped to shreds, never given a chance, by the children in their homes. One boy, in a counseling session with his mother, said of his stepfather, "The guy is a total asshole. I can't believe you got together with him. What do you know about him, anyway? Did you ever think about hiring a private detective to trail him for a while? You might find out some stuff you're not going to like." His mother was devastated.

Another boy had become used to "talking fresh" to his mother, in a sassy, somewhat defiant way that she elected to ignore. Suddenly, a rather authoritarian stepfather entered the picture, came to the mother's defense, and told her son he wasn't to talk to his mom that way. To which the son replied, "You might be married to her, but you're not my father. Actually, you're nothing to me, so you can't tell me what to do."

Typically, we might think it's the four- or five-year-old who's given to shouting, "You're not my real dad" or "You're not my real mom." But adolescents can and do launch exactly the same verbal attacks; in addition, they have the capacity to act out in acutely hurtful ways, designed to upset the biological parent and prove to the stepparent how powerless he or she is. Acting out often takes the form of increasingly dangerous secretive behaviors—such as drinking, drugging, or, as with Maggie, having sex with a lot of boys. When Mom confronts her, the teen answers, in effect, "Well, why do you care? It's not like you're my mother anymore, you're more interested in being with him. When I had a mother, then maybe I would listen to you, but why should I listen to you now?" Maggie was getting back at her mom and being highly strategic in how she went about it.

If you find yourself embroiled in this kind of standoff with your teen, first keep in mind that it's really not about you. As determined as your child may seem to drive a stake through your heart, acting out verbal or physical behaviors is about the child's difficulty in coming to grips with the changes in her life—changes she didn't have any real say over. A parent, quite understandably, rarely says to a child something like, "You know, I've been dating Frank for a year now, and I like him a lot. How would you feel about my marrying him?"—giving her, in a sense, a little heads-up about what's coming and suggesting that she, the teen, is in the loop. Typically, however, the marriage happens, and Mom says, "I know you'll get to like him," which sounds completely lame to a resentful teenager. Anyway, maybe she *won't* get to like her mother's new husband because he's not very likable.

Second, address the standoff head-on. When an adolescent is pretty far along in acting-out behaviors, such as having sex with several partners, it may be wise to invest in a brief stretch of family counseling: Maggie, her mother, her sister, and her stepfather could benefit from talking over their differences with a helpful third party. In addition, Maggie's mother needs to reassert her bonds with her daughter—maybe by spending more time together, or getting better at listening, or letting her new husband know Maggie needs to be her priority for a while. Although on the surface it didn't seem so, Maggie was probably feeling deserted.

Other times, reasserting your bonds with your new spouse, and letting your child know that you and that individual are speaking with one voice, is needed. An adolescent resists being controlled; someone controlling you who isn't even your parent becomes an obvious target for attack: "You're nothing to me, you can't tell me what to do."

Ideally, all these potential pitfalls will be negotiated between the two new partners before things get ugly. Creating a parenting partnership for a blended family that includes adolescents is a real challenge.

Single parenting can be even harder, because a mother or father lacks the stamina and support, or the tag-team ability, of two parents ("You go talk to him. I can't deal with him right now"). In addition, when resources—time, money, energy—are stretched thin, it's difficult to provide the structure an adolescent needs if secretive behaviors are looking dangerous. When it's only you, parenting is tough. That's especially when the need for a community endeavor is apparent, in the form of other sensible and helpful adults.

Find parenting peers.

The divorced mother of a sixteen-year-old noted that as the years went by, "I talked to fewer and fewer other parents. I was mostly among other people like me right after my son was born, and a bunch of us from the Lamaze group kept in touch. So about six or seven or us moms would sit around somebody's living room nursing our babies, talking about cracked nipples and all that. Then I met some mothers through those little toddler classes we went to—all the Mommy and Me stuff. Early elementary school was pretty good, because there were school fairs, visiting days, holiday plays, and you had chances to meet other parents. The last few years, there hasn't been a lot of contact. At my son's school, we're each asked to volunteer one day a semester to go on parent patrol, so you put on an orange vest and you and another parent walk around the neighborhood for an hour or so after classes let out that day. So for an hour I talk to another mother or father. I think we all could probably clue each other in on stuff that's going on with our kids, but nobody really gets together much."

The widowed father of a twelve-year-old said his son's school instituted a parents-in-action program: "We all sat around in a circle this one evening, there was a 'facilitator' who was supposed to suggest issues or keep the talk productive. And I guess it was productive, except that two parents whose kids were having a lot of problems kept monopolizing the discussion around specific gripes they had, or things they thought the school should handle differently. I went to two of these meetings. Then the third one was postponed indefinitely, and that was the end of that."

Getting together with the parents of other adolescents is an excellent idea—even if you're not a single parent. But the experiences of this mother and father demonstrate some of the barriers to that effort. Once into the middle school years and beyond, there do tend to be fewer school-based opportunities to hang around with other adults and swap stories, and of course Mom is no longer in charge of arranging playdates and so at least spending some time on the phone with other moms. Parents-in-action type sessions, which are great ideas, rapidly fall by the wayside. People find it difficult to make time for them; people sense that the event is dominated by one or two parents with "issues," and that produces resentment or the feeling that such meetings are designed for the troubled few.

We'd all be better served to acknowledge this fact about raising adolescents: Everyone has difficulty with his or her kids; everyone has issues. And if you don't, then you don't know enough about what's really going on. Many teens, of course, sail through these years quite successfully, but it is in the nature of the beast to stir up conflict, as part of asserting independence and "otherness."

Your child's life is moving way too fast for you to absorb information all on your own. You, in turn, need avenues of reference and support and feedback, because of these three normal adolescent impulses.

Teenagers work at keeping adults in the dark. Simply the terminology teens use can be a mystery, which is the way they'd like it to remain. For example, I've learned from children that the current word for being stoned on ecstasy is "rolling." Who knew? But it's easy to imagine the following conversation between a parent and her child:

Mom: "Good morning, did you have fun last night with your friends?"

Teen: "Yeah, we were really rolling."

Mom: "Oh, good, I'm glad you had a nice time."

Teen, thinking to himself: *Yeah, duh, if you only knew what I just said, ha! Good one on you, Mom.*

Teenagers prefer that parents not talk to other parents. Your child may fight ferociously against any alliance you have with her friend's mothers and fathers. She believes it's in her best interests to discourage fraternization among the elders.

Teenagers enjoy wearing adults down. And they have many ideas, including some gained from the media and popular culture, on how to exhaust their parents and outwit the system. Also, they make good use of our tendency to be a little slow on the uptake. Some years ago I worked with the personnel in a local high school, who had just instituted a new rule: If a student missed school, a note to that effect would be sent home with the child the following day; the note was to be signed by his parents and returned to the teacher. On day one, each student was given a form and told, "Take this home and have your parents sign it, so we will have their signatures on record for future comparison." This well-meaning strategy was defeated in about one minute, which was how long it took the teenagers to realize they could sign the forms themselves and all future signatures would match perfectly. It took the school about a year to figure that out.

All this is by way of saying, do keep communicating with other parents. Maybe it's possible to set up, informally, a talk group such as described by the father I just mentioned. I see this as a way of enhancing community and broadening understanding, not just targeting problem children or even the difficulties of parenting. Mothers and fathers need each other to navigate these years, and everyone benefits from the feeling of comradeship and the reality of going through a particular stage of children's lives together—just as, perhaps, you did with your fellow Lamaze mothers years ago. Talking to your parent peers, you may have a few so-*that's*-what-that-word-means moments.

You may be thinking, *Yes, there's some stuff I don't know about my child's activities or I wonder about, and I'd like to get together with some other parents, compare notes, because that will help.* To which I add: It's not even what you know you don't know; there's a lot you *don't know* you don't know, and that's where parent peers can be invaluable.

And they can be more than a source of feedback, information, and comparing notes. Especially if you're into Stage 2 parenting on your own, you need people to support you as a parent while you do what you must do with your child—people who might sometimes give you a hug, and say, "That was hard, what you just went through with your kid. You're doing a terrific job."

Parenting Substitutes for Your Teenager

When she was eleven, Lynne went to sleepaway camp for four weeks that summer and had a miserable time of it for the first two. During those two weeks, she mailed home many pitiful letters describing her misery: "I hate it here! How many times does it take to tell you that! Could you take off three or four days from my stay here? I miss you so much. Please come for me." Lynne's concerned and caring parents kept in regular phone contact with the camp director and their daughter's cabin counselor, and were reassured that overall Lynne was fitting in nicely, making a few friends, and participating in sports, and that the misery seemed to descend only sporadically, just before she fell asleep. They decided it would be good for Lynne to stick it out. During the second half of summer camp, her parents heard virtually nothing from their child. When they went to collect her at the end, Lynne was in tears at having to leave her wonderful new friends and her wonderful camp.

Her parents mentioned this, to them, amusing story to now

fifteen-year-old Lynne, who was annoyed. "And why, exactly, is that something you feel a need to bring up?" she said. Her parents thought she'd have a chuckle over the long-ago incident, and maybe when she's twenty-five, she will. At the moment, as she was developing her identity and pursuing her private life, she'd rather not be reminded of certain things, and it wasn't a plus that her parents had that information.

At this age, your child does not want to be transparent, known, and predictable. One boy put the feeling this way: "My parents are pretty cool, but the problem is, they knew me when I was a little kid. That's why I don't want to tell them a lot of stuff." He was saying, "The person they're relating to is the person I used to be, and I'm not that person anymore." Teenagers insist, "I'm grown up now," but even they are able to acknowledge they're not all *that* grown up. What they are, however, is different from the way they were, and they believe their parents don't get it.

It's also true that during these years, your child is searching for different models of how people respond to ideas and situations. In a sense, she actively craves contact with people who are unlikely to react the way you do; once she starts predicting your reactions with regularity or some accuracy, she sees less point in communicating with you. Often, I ask an adolescent, "Didn't you tell your mom about that?" And she replies, "Nah, I know what she'd say." Even if it might be good advice, her thought is, *Why bother?* She wants to hear from someone with another idea— which is not just, "I want to talk to somebody who'll tell me that the sneaky thing I did is okay," although there may be some of that. Mainly, she seeks the input of a person who may see the same situation in a different way from you.

These sensibilities are what often cause a teen to find it easier to share her thoughts with someone who didn't know her back when (even four years ago), or someone who might have an unexpected slant on issues. If your child has such an individual in her life—a favorite uncle or aunt, the youth leader at church or synagogue, a sports coach—that's a wonderful achievement. If she doesn't, look around; think of another adult you all know with whom she can develop rapport and encourage that connection. From a developmental standpoint, it's really not possible for your adolescent to turn to you with all her cares and woes, questions and observations.

Sometimes, it makes sense for a child, even before age eighteen, to live somewhere else for a while. On a number of occasions, I have met with a parent who presents some version of the following: "We moved here because of my husband's job at the end of our son's sophomore year in high school. He really loved it back in Arizona where we used to live, and he's been kind of a mess here for the first half of junior year. So he's going to go back and live with his best friend's parents for the rest of the year, and maybe even to finish out high school." These in loco parentis arrangements can work well, if everyone is in agreement and sometimes—if a child has been in therapy—after consultation with a professional. In general, these sorts of separations need a great deal of discussion and should have clear time limits attached to them.

Adolescents are constantly pushing the notion that their parents don't understand them, don't appreciate that they're growing up and they're not little kids anymore. And I say, "Yes, we'll work very hard to help your parents understand that you're different now than you used to be. But you know what? You have to try to understand that your parents aren't the same people they used to be, either. They're older, they have shorter attention spans, their memory isn't so hot anymore. They're losing their hair or putting on weight. They're worried about bills and getting you through college. They're frightened. Sometimes they look at you, and all they can think about are drugs and drinking and pregnancy and jail terms. These people are changing too!"

It's an effort to promote acknowledgment that Stage 2 parenting is tough on everybody involved. My message in this chapter: The more we adults can pull together through all the inevitable changes as life goes on, the better we'll be able to meet them.

You and Your Teenager

What a Perfect Relationship Looks Like
Isn't That Everything Goes Perfectly

A sociologist once defined adolescence as the time between when a child thinks he should be treated as an adult and when he is, in fact, an adult. It starts with that change in attitude: the sense of entitlement to privacy and secrets that your child acquires seemingly overnight when he crosses the Rubicon into prepuberty and puberty. On the one hand, he's not a little kid anymore. On the other hand, he's not a grown-up yet. In a nutshell, that's what makes these years, for parents, newly stressful, exhausting, and exhilarating all at once. It also encapsulates the theme that has been running through all the strategies I've suggested in *I Can't Believe You Went Through My Stuff!*

On the one hand, as often as possible, deal with your teenager as if he were the adult he wishes to be. Put your money where your mouth is; if you want him to start acting like an adult—by assuming responsibility for his actions and making informed and intelligent decisions concerning his behaviors—start treating him like one. Some years back, Erma Bombeck wrote a column in which she speculated on how it would seem if our next-door neighbors came over for dinner and we spoke to them the way we speak to our children: "Did you wash your face before you came? Don't tell me your hands are clean, I saw you playing with the dog. Sit up straight. Use your napkin and don't talk with food in your mouth." It was a small plea for extending to children a measure of the courtesy we offer our fellow grown-ups—partly by refraining from pointing out all they're getting wrong while failing to acknowledge what they're getting right, and partly by believing they're capable of figuring some stuff out for themselves.

Many of the parent-to-child conversations, or conversation starters, that I have described are based on this premise: Assume adulthood. Appeal to your child's higher self, or his capacity to reason and his wish to do the right thing. (There's always time to backtrack and deal with a secretive situation that's become worrisome by realizing that, at the moment, you're confronting the little kid in your child.) Offer your adolescent a way to prove himself to you. Allow him some privacy and some space. If he abuses it, you'll do something about that, but start by assuming that he won't.

On the other hand, a twelve-, fourteen-, or sixteen-year-old is still a child, which means she needs guidance and a great deal of patience. Many parents acquire something of a what's-in-this-for-me? attitude, especially during those times an adolescent is being anything but gratifying to them. This is when Mom or Dad thinks, *I go to great lengths to be available to my kid. I talk to her helpfully, I turn down things I'd like to do in order to be home for her, and she treats me like an obnoxious intruder. What about my needs, my need to feel like an effective parent? What about my need to enjoy life a little more?* Then, when the teen acts "childish," Mom or Dad says, "I'm so disappointed in you. I thought you were a lot more grown up than that."

I have said that often we expect teenagers to be much more

advanced than they are, and we're inclined to promote them to adulthood before they're ready—sometimes for our convenience and sometimes out of frustration and weariness. In addition, the cultural paradigm of adolescents is that they're trouble, they're going to wear us down, we might as well give up early. It *is* time-consuming to have to keep providing structure in the form of rules and consequences, double checking and following up, and so on. Yet that's an inescapable aspect of Stage 2 parenting. Adolescents at some level don't *want* their parents to give up on the more onerous parts of the job; they don't want to be tortured, but they don't want to be abandoned, either.

All this is about the need to walk that fine line between stepping back and letting your child solve his "Who am I?" dilemma according to his own lights, and stepping in when he needs your advice and protection. It takes time to walk the line. And it takes keeping on your toes—not because you must be supersuspicious about everything, but because cultural influences combined with the typical teen's emotional and psychological lability may call for many parental midcourse corrections. The responses you make must be incremental. It's like looking toward the horizon; you can't see closer to the end without moving up a little farther. You can't know ten steps, much less two years, down the road before you get through what's right in front of you.

Some teens follow a fairly linear developmental pattern, when things happen pretty much when they're supposed to happen. Others seem to be walking in place for long stretches, then make giant surges forward. But during Stage 2 parenting, all adolescents become somewhat unfamiliar to their parents. Adolescents see their lives as great dramas-in-progress; they often discuss their feelings and experiences in melodramatic terms, even when all is relatively sunny. A girl told me, "I know I have a wonderful life. My parents are terrific, they're so understanding. But God, it's still so hard, they really don't know."

In the midst of all this Sturm und Drang, you cannot be complacent. Vigilance is the normal status of the parent of a teenager.

However, now that I've made the case for remaining on heightened alert, I would add, Go easy on yourself. You can feel encouraged, confident, and hopeful, for several reasons.

You're Probably Doing Better than You Think

Or better than you feel at any given moment. You're probably helping your teen internalize important controls even when it least seems so.

Fourteen-year-old Nell desperately wanted to attend a rock concert in another town, two hours away on the freeway. Nell assured her mother that she would be riding with her friend Chrissie; Chrissie's older brother, who got his driver's license two weeks earlier; and the brother's friend. "The concert starts at eight, and we'll be back at two," said Nell. "No, I don't think so," said her mother.

Nell: "But Mom, everybody's going! I can't have a life?"

Mom: "Look, the boys may be nice, but they haven't been driving very long. It'll be dark at the concert. I'm sure there will be people selling drugs. You could easily get separated or lost, and the boys might not be able to protect you."

Furious, Nell stormed upstairs to her room and slammed the door. Her mother's feelings were a little hurt, but she said nothing more.

Half an hour later, Nell's mother went upstairs and overheard her daughter talking on the phone: "I know, but your brother's only been driving a couple of weeks. And there probably will be drug dealers there . . ."

Adolescents do have an inflated sense of their own invulnerability and a persistent need to demonstrate that their parents don't understand and can't tell them anything. But they also do want to survive and thrive, and they'd prefer not to let their parents down. Like Nell, they will hear and heed a mother's or father's wisdom—even if they don't want to admit it.

That's not to say that you will always sound wise or that you will not find yourself spouting somewhat inane arguments at times. Especially when you're suggesting, calmly and rationally, that it's not advisable to smoke, or sneak in and out of the house, or cut school, and your child comes back at you with, "Well, you probably did the same thing when you were my age." I remember such conversations with my teenage children and my responding with the words my parents said to me and probably every parent since the dawn of time has said: "That was different!" And my son or daughter responding the way every parent's son or daughter would: "How?" And then hearing my answer ("I was older; the beer was weak; my brother was there; the cigarettes were cheap; the teachers were meaner") and realizing as these explanations were flying out of my mouth, *This is jibberish! I'm making this up as I go along! I'm fighting for my life here!*

But overall, considering the hundreds of large and small messages you convey by careful listening and thoughtful responding, you're almost certainly running up many more pluses than minuses. A lot of what you're doing may be working very well, even though you don't see it working in the heat of the moment.

It's Not All So Serious

I sometimes say to the nervous parents of teenagers, "If we put a hidden camera in your household, filmed your life for a couple of days, and showed the results to an audience, mostly they'd laugh." A lot of what goes on in a family is funny, and laughing at yourself now and then is a good thing.

There's a distinction we find hard to remember when living with adolescents, which is that although many issues are important, not everything is serious. Important or significant issues can still be treated lightly or in a positive way. But parents as a rule take things way too seriously; we just refuse to have any sense of humor about what's going on with a child, fearing that letting up for a second means condoning all kinds of mischief and danger. It doesn't.

Often, when I hear a boy or girl describe some fairly outrageous bit of activity he or she has been up to—he pulled the wool over his dad's eyes by sneaking out in the car; she gave her mom a fit by showing up with a boy who looked like a thug—my feeling is, you sort of have to admire that! No, it wasn't a great thing to do, and yes, the behavior should change, but here's a young person demonstrating a little zest and derring-do. Any adolescent who's at all active will push the boundaries. Sometimes our response (at least to ourselves) needs to be, "Good one!"

Time Is on Your Side

All parents at some point feel they're in over their heads with their teenager. But the secret weapon in getting your child to adulthood is the passage of time. Sometimes what you must do is keep your child reasonably steady while maturity catches up to him. Even the most turbulent behavior often just irons out in time.

Fortunately, you do have a few more options available to you than simply living in hope that your teen will survive eventually. It's all right to believe that a child's uncomfortable or difficult experience will be like yours, and since you got through it, so will he. But you don't need to squander your ability to problem-solve with your adolescent when difficulties do come up. The strategies I've talked about in this book are helpful actions to take, while the passage of time is wielding its good effect.

Mostly, It All Winds Up Nicely in the End

It's not uncommon for parents to want to have it all, to have a perfect relationship with their child. But what a perfect relationship looks like isn't that everything goes perfectly. People who are mentally healthy aren't people with no problems; they're people who are willing to face the problems they have.

Your child will have his or her share of problems; he or she has to go through that stage. We know that teens who spend a lot of time in jail or who lose themselves in substance abuse do face a greater likelihood of difficulties later in life. Other than that, however, there is not much correlation between how stressful one's adolescence is and how much one succeeds or fails as an adult. We all know friends who say, "Boy, I was a mess when I was a teenager, I really struggled with my parents, but it came out all right."

My hypothesis is: That struggle is required, in some form or other. And you have the power to help your son or daughter by being willing and able to accept the struggle as a necessary part of his or her development.

Index

abandonment, fear of, 83

abuse, physical, 90, 129, 131, 202

Alateen, 154, 205

alcohol abuse

　evidence of, 151

　expressing suspicion about, 151

　family history of, 151

　parents' denial of, 150

　prevalence of, 150

　seeking help for, 151–52

　surveys about, 181

Alcoholics Anonymous, 154

alcoholism, parental, 202

alcohol use

　evidence of, finding, 107

　evidence of, reacting to, 117

　inquiring about, 69, 88–89

　minimizing opportunity for,
　　106, 188

　parents' need to know about, 90

allowance, 180–81

anger, parental, 178, 192, 216, 217

anger, teen, 133, 164, 192–93

anxiety, 74–75, 164, 217

appearance, concern about, 84–85

artistic talents, 30, 31

assault, definition of, 145

bedrooms

　establishing rules about, 104–5

　finding alarming items in, 107

　finding drugs in, 148

　as sanctuary, 11–12

snooping in, 104–5, 148

Being Adolescent (Csikszentmihalyi
　and Larson), 11

birth control pills, 112

bodily hygiene, 60–61

Bombeck, Erma, 229–30

boundaries, setting, 95–96, 210

boyfriends, inquiring about, 72–75

brain development, 15–16

bullying, by teens, 132–33

bullying, of teens

　case study, 128–31

　fear felt by victims, 129–30

　handling, suggestions for, 132,
　　134–37

　inquiring about, 128–29

　parents' need to know about, 90

　parents' reaction to, 131

　shame felt by victims, 130–31

　supportive measures for, 132

　warning signs of, 131

bullying prevention programs,
　136

case studies

　Andy: abusing drugs, 147–49

　Jack: bullied teen, 128–31

　Jen: cutting herself, 159–62

　Marcy: Internet romance,
　　137–39

cell phones, 104

chat rooms, 122, 138, 144

cigarettes, 88–89, 109, 181